GOOD CATCH

University Press of Florida

Florida A&M University, Tallahassee • Florida Atlantic University, Boca Raton
Florida Gulf Coast University, Ft. Myers • Florida International University, Miami
Florida State University, Tallahassee • New College of Florida, Sarasota
University of Central Florida, Orlando • University of Florida, Gainesville
University of North Florida, Jacksonville • University of South Florida, Tampa
University of West Florida, Pensacola

GOOD CATCH

RECIPES & STORIES
celebrating the best of
FLORIDA'S WATERS

PAM BRANDON
KATIE FARMAND
and
HEATHER McPHERSON

PHOTOGRAPHY BY
DIANA ZALUCKY

University Press of Florida
Gainesville/Tallahassee/Tampa/Boca Raton
Pensacola/Orlando/Miami/Jacksonville/Ft. Myers/Sarasota

VIVA FLORIDA 500.
1513-2013

A FLORIDA QUINCENTENNIAL BOOK

Copyright 2014 by Pam Brandon, Katie Farmand,
and Heather McPherson
Photography copyright 2014 by Diana Zalucky
All rights reserved
Design by Jason Farmand
Illustrations by Melissa Huerta
All photos are by Diana Zalucky unless otherwise
stated on page 277.
Printed in China on acid-free paper

19 18 17 16 15 14   6 5 4 3 2 1

Library of Congress Control Number: 2014934340
ISBN 978-0-8130-6015-6

The University Press of Florida is the scholarly
publishing agency for the State University System
of Florida, comprising Florida A&M University,
Florida Atlantic University, Florida Gulf Coast
University, Florida International University, Florida
State University, New College of Florida, University
of Central Florida, University of Florida, University
of North Florida, University of South Florida, and
University of West Florida.

University Press of Florida
15 Northwest 15th Street
Gainesville, FL 32611-2079
http://www.upf.com

TO OUR FAMILIES,
AND TO THE HARD-WORKING
FARMERS OF THE SEA

Contents

AN ABBREVIATED VISUAL GUIDE TO

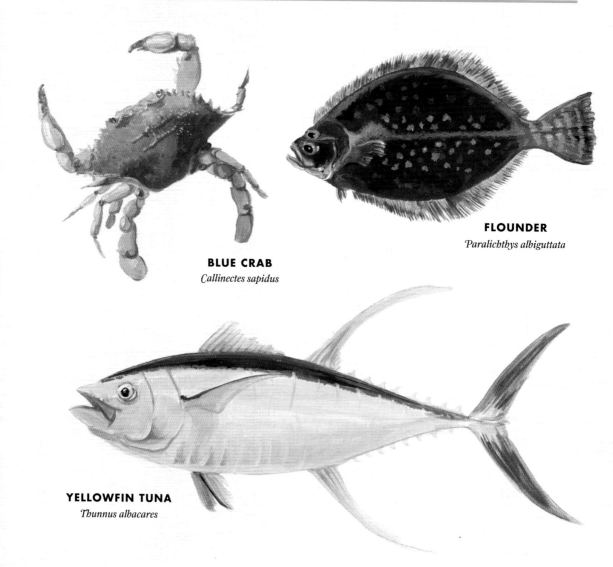

FLOUNDER
Paralichthys albiguttata

BLUE CRAB
Callinectes sapidus

YELLOWFIN TUNA
Thunnus albacares

PINK SHRIMP
Mycteroperca bonaci

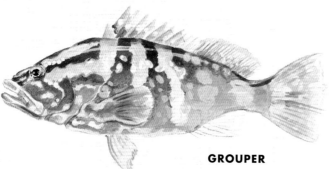

GROUPER
Epinephelus morio

Florida's COMMON SEAFOOD

ILLUSTRATED BY MELISSA HUERTA

POMPANO
Trachinotus carolinus

RED SNAPPER
Lutjunus campechanus

SPINY LOBSTER
Panulirus argus

SWORDFISH
Xiphias gladius

MAHI MAHI
Coryphaena hippurus

INTRODUCTION

Up at daybreak, we're out on a boat in the mind-blowing wilds of the Ten Thousand Islands, and it is love at first sight. A manatee and her baby, nostrils peeking out of the water for a breath of fresh air, sidle up to our slow-moving craft. Minutes later a pod of bottlenose dolphins puts on an impromptu ballet. And before noon, we snag a silvery tarpon on our fishing line, then let it slip away. Ah, just another day at the office.

Good Catch is an expansion of our first book, Field to Feast, recipes and stories from Florida farms that took us from the Panhandle to Homestead. We intended to include seafood in that book until we realized the impossibility of showcasing both land and sea in a finite number of pages. So we headed back on the road, this time following two-lane blacktop through wetlands and hammocks to eat onion rings and fried mullet at rustic fish camps, slurp oysters in Apalachicola, and dig into

AND BEFORE NOON, WE SNAG A SILVERY TARPON ON OUR FISHING LINE, THEN LET IT SLIP AWAY. AH, JUST ANOTHER DAY AT THE OFFICE.

steamed spiny lobster in the Florida Keys. We
trailed a meandering boardwalk over sand dunes
late one afternoon to witness a catch of the day in
the tumbling Atlantic Ocean. On the Miami River,
we met weathered Cuban fishermen on a dock
where time stands still. And on the Gulf Coast, we
marveled at shells no bigger than the head of a pin in
the palm of a clam farmer's hand.

Surrounded by water on three sides with an
inland maze of lakes, rivers, streams, and springs,
the largest lake in the Southeast plunked in the
middle, and the Everglades seeping out below, all of
Florida is alive with watery abundance—life that has
nourished humans on this peninsula for centuries
and today helps feed much of the world.

And while there's unspoken camaraderie among
fishermen, coaxing out a story isn't always easy. They
live quietly on the water, often away at sea for days
at a time to bring a backbreaking load of sustenance
to shore. But there is pride in their hard work, and
the joy that comes with the freedom of spending
time so very close to nature. The passion often starts
early in life with the first cast of a line, a frog gigged,
or a net full of shrimp. When you champion a local
fisherman, you are supporting a way of life that
has survived for generations in little towns such as
Tarpon Springs, Cortez, Aripeka, and Amelia Island.

This book is presented by season, as so much of Florida seafood is abundant only at certain times of the year. We know oysters are best in "r" months, and scallop season is July through September. We learned that amberjack is most prolific on the Southwest Coast in winter, mahi mahi is an easy summer catch in the Keys, cobia is abundant in the spring in the Gulf, and the season for snook on the Atlantic Coast is in the fall.

In the kitchen, we discovered new tastes like bottarga, the cured roe of mullet. We tentatively filleted our first snapper and packed a sheepshead in coarse salt to roast it to buttery tenderness. We shucked and roasted oysters, steamed clams, and grilled octopus. Conch fritters, shrimp, and frog legs were perfectly fried. And we did our best to even out the calories with plenty of seasonal salads and side dishes to accompany the wealth of seafood and take advantage of Florida's abundant crops.

So dive in for a taste of the bounty of Florida. We hope this book brings to life the watery world of our beautiful state.

Spring's
BOUNTY

RIMP • COBIA • RED DRUM • SHEEPSHEAD • ... • CUCUMBERS • BLUEBERRIES • PE...

RED SHRIMP • COBIA • RED DRUM • SHEEPSHEAD • ZUCCHINI • CARROTS • CUCUMBERS • BLUEBERRI

SPARKLING WHITE SANGRIA

| MAKES 4¼ CUPS |

¼ cup fresh mint leaves

¼ cup sugar

¼ cup water

1 (750-ml) bottle sparkling white wine

1 cup Lillet Rosé

2 large or 4 small Florida peaches, pitted and sliced

½ pint Florida blueberries, halved

EFFERVESCENT AND FRUITY, this sangria gets a little kick from Lillet Rosé, a dry French aperitif. Florida peach season is just three months, March through May, so plan to enjoy this cocktail during balmy spring evenings with a light seafood dinner. An inexpensive sparkler is best for this—try an Italian prosecco or Spanish cava.

1 Combine mint, sugar, and water in a small saucepan over medium-high heat. Bring to a simmer, stirring until sugar dissolves. Remove from heat, cover, and let steep 20 minutes. Refrigerate mint simple syrup until cold, about 1 hour. Discard mint.

2 Combine mint simple syrup, sparkling wine, rosé, peaches, and blueberries in a large pitcher, stirring to combine. Serve immediately over ice.

ROSEWATER COLLINS »

| MAKES 1 DRINK |

2 ounces gin, such as Hendrick's

2 to 3 teaspoons simple syrup

3 thin slices peeled cucumber

2 fresh lime wedges

3 to 4 drops rosewater

Ice

Sparkling water

Cucumber spears and fresh rose petals, for serving

LIKE A SPRING GARDEN IN A GLASS, floral rosewater, fragrant gin, and refreshing cucumber are a light and lovely trio perfectly suited for a light appetizer like our Cobia Crudo with Chiles and Mint. To make simple syrup, combine equal parts sugar and water in a pan and cook until sugar dissolves. Cool completely before using and refrigerate in an airtight container for up to 1 week.

1 Combine gin, simple syrup, cucumber, lime wedge, rosewater, and ice in a cocktail shaker. Shake vigorously for about 10 seconds.

2 Strain mixture into a glass and top with sparkling water. Garnish with a cucumber spear and a rose petal.

ROYAL RED SHRIMP SALAD

| SERVES 6 |

EVERY SPRING, WE EAGERLY ANTICIPATE the first delivery of royal red shrimp to our local seafood market. Virtually unknown until a decade ago, this crimson-hued shrimp variety can be found around the whole perimeter of Florida—and they are usually netted somewhere around a half-mile deep. Because of their dark environment and higher fat content, royal reds have a texture that's closer to that of lobster, and their flavor is sweet and briny. Because of their delicate texture, royal red shrimp need only a very brief dip in boiling water. They're ideal for a quick weeknight supper, steamed or sautéed, but they're also incredibly delicious tossed in this light dressing and served cold. However you prefer, they are a seasonal treat we are always excited to see.

2 pounds large royal red shrimp, peeled and deveined

2 tablespoons extra-virgin olive oil, divided

1 teaspoon finely grated fresh lemon zest

2 tablespoons fresh lemon juice

2 tablespoons mayonnaise

2 tablespoons chopped fresh dill

1 (14-ounce) can hearts of palm, thinly sliced

1 medium red bell pepper, seeded and finely diced

¼ cup finely diced red onion

Coarse salt and freshly ground black pepper, to taste

HOW TO PEEL AND DEVEIN SHRIMP

Pull off heads if still attached. Remove legs, cracking shell in the bottom center. Starting at the head end, peel away shells. Depending on the way you want to serve the shrimp, you can leave the last segment and tail or remove them. Use a small, sharp knife to cut a slit down the back of shrimp about ¼-inch deep. Remove and discard the vein under cold running water or use the tip of a knife.

1 Bring a large pot of water to a boil. Add shrimp, stir, and remove with a slotted spoon after 1 minute. Set aside to cool.

2 Whisk together oil, lemon zest and juice, mayonnaise, and dill. Add shrimp, hearts of palm, red bell pepper, and onion, tossing to coat. Season to taste with salt and pepper.

3 Cover tightly and refrigerate at least 4 hours and up to overnight.

BAKED OYSTERS with BUTTER, GARLIC, and PARMESAN CHEESE

| MAKES 2 DOZEN |

½ cup softened unsalted butter

½ cup freshly grated Parmesan cheese

2 garlic cloves, finely minced

1 tablespoon fresh lemon juice

1 tablespoon chopped fresh parsley

Hot sauce, to taste

2 dozen oysters on the half shell

INDIAN PASS RAW BAR IN PORT ST. JOE has a simple menu and a simple system: oysters, crabs, shrimp, gumbo, and cold drinks—all on the honor system. It became a restaurant in 1986, but in 1903, the building was a commissary for a turpentine company. During the Great Depression, it was home to a store, gas station, and restaurant that housed the spectacularly named Gypsie McNeill's Tearoom. Today, Gypsie's grandson runs the restaurant.

To get to the seafood shack you must travel a long, remote stretch of county road between Apalachicola and Port St. Joe. Just when you think you're lost, a small yellow sign appears along the roadside warning of "congestion ahead." Be ready to tap the brakes because just around a slight curve is the raw bar, surrounded by people sipping beer on the porch and cars jockeying for parking spots.

Pull into the gravel lot and head to the door. There will likely be a wait list, but be sure to scope out the bar seats. Often there are one or two open near the back. Grab a beer from the cooler and revel in the chaos. If you catch the eye of a server, holler out your order and settle in. Despite the ongoing bustle, this is not fast food.

The oysters at Indian Pass Raw Bar are so fresh, many guests prefer to slurp them down raw on the half shell. For those who prefer a cooked bivalve, the baked oysters are an incredibly rich and full-flavored indulgence.

1 Place oven rack 5 to 6 inches from heat source and preheat broiler.

2 Combine butter, Parmesan, garlic, lemon juice, parsley, and hot sauce in a small bowl.

3 Place raw oysters in a single layer in a baking dish and evenly distribute butter mixture over them.

4 Broil until oysters begin to curl at the edges and butter mixture is bubbly, 5 to 7 minutes.

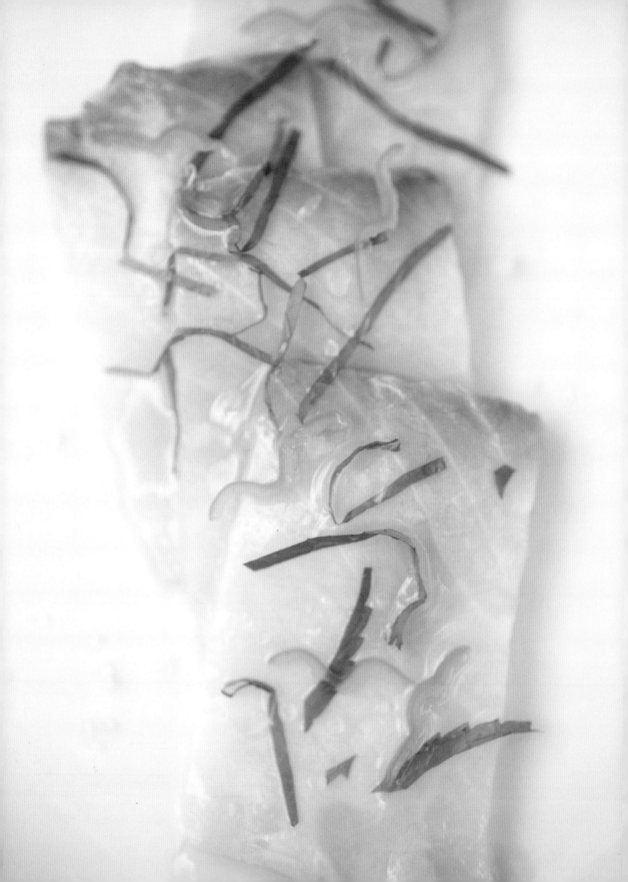

COBIA CRUDO with CHILES and MINT

| SERVES 4 |

THERE ARE SO MANY FACTORS experienced anglers consider before heading out to fish. Bait choice, time of day, and weather all play a part, but cobia enthusiasts know that temperature might be the most important factor for finding the highly valued fish. Cobia migrate south in the fall as the water temperatures drop and swim north in the spring as the water warms up, so fishermen wait for the "sweet spot"—when the water in the Gulf or the Atlantic is between 68°F and 72°F. That's when you'll find the popular game fish.

Cobia's mild flavor makes it a darling of chefs—it's delicious simply seared but also works well in more elaborate preparations. Its buttery, firm texture allows it to be grilled, baked, seared, or even eaten raw, which is our favorite way to enjoy this tasty saltwater catch.

This simple preparation allows the flavor and texture of the cobia to really shine. If you aren't using fish you caught yourself, let your fishmonger know you'll be serving this raw so he will give you the freshest fish and best cut available. Keep the fish very cold before slicing and use a narrow, sharp knife to get thin, even slices. And if you can't find a Meyer lemon, regular lemon or even lime juice will do.

½ pound skinless cobia fillet

2 to 3 teaspoons fresh Meyer lemon juice

1 small fresh habanero chile, seeded and thinly sliced

4 fresh mint leaves, thinly sliced

4 teaspoons good-quality fruity extra-virgin olive oil

Coarse sea salt

1 Slice cobia into ¼-inch-thick slices and arrange on a serving plate.

2 Sprinkle lemon juice over fish, then evenly distribute chiles and mint over the top. Drizzle with oil and sprinkle with salt. Serve immediately.

TED PETERS FAMOUS SMOKED FISH SPREAD

| MAKES ABOUT 2 CUPS |

YOU SMELL IT BEFORE YOU SEE IT. An authentic slice of old Florida, Ted Peters Famous Smoked Fish is a Gulf Coast landmark along busy Pasadena Avenue in St. Petersburg. It's easy to find—just follow your nose to the rich aroma of seafood smoking over a smoldering red oak fire.

Grab a seat at one of the outdoor picnic tables, a wooden stool at the counter, or a chair in the small dining room, and you'll see patrons diving into big plates of smoked mahi mahi, mackerel, salmon, and mullet with sides of warm German potato salad, coleslaw, and a slab of sweet onion. This is mecca for smoked fish fans, with more than 100,000 pounds of fish smoked each year in an adjacent shack.

Ted Peters got into the smoked fish business in the late 1940s, when he salvaged an old smoker he found. Ted started smoking mullet right on the side of the two-lane road where people could see it, smell it, and jam on the brakes. By 1951, Ted Peters Famous Smoked Fish was in business in the same location as today, though the road is now a busy six-lane highway. Generations of families have grown up eating the smoked fish, says co-owner Mike Lathrop, the founder's nephew, who has been there for more than forty years.

Torpedo-shaped striped mullet, a plentiful catch along the Gulf Coast, spends most of their time close to shore near streams and rivers, or in brackish bays, inlets, and lagoons, and is the star of the show. Thick slabs of the raw fish are salted, lightly seasoned, and laid on racks over a smoldering fire of red oak, a tree native to Florida that's similar to northern hickory. The oily fish is smoked from four to six hours, depending on its size and thickness. Five generations after the business's founding, the process is nearly perfected, with Ben Cook, Ted's great-grandson, now smoking the fish.

The restaurant has added a hefty burger to the fishcentric menu, and now a new generation of regulars order the Ted Peters version of "surf 'n' turf": the restaurant's fluffy, hand-mixed fish spread, a side of saltines, and a cheeseburger. Mike shares their recipe for the fish spread.

¾ cup smoked mahi mahi

¾ cup smoked mullet

½ cup sweet pickle relish with pimiento

½ cup salad dressing (such as Miracle Whip)

¼ cup finely diced onion

¼ cup finely diced celery

Coarse salt and freshly ground black pepper, to taste

1 Flake fish into fine pieces and combine with remaining ingredients in a mixing bowl.

2 Cover and refrigerate until ready to serve. Fluff with fork before serving.

RED DRUM with OLIVE SAUCE

| SERVES 2 |

IF YOU'RE LUCKY ENOUGH TO SNAG a spot on Lawrence Piper's boat, you'll see a side of Northeast Florida that few really know. Part fish whisperer, part instructor, part nature guide, Lawrence takes charters into the Intracoastal waterways, creeks, and marshes around Amelia Island. "There are a whole lot of people who can fish better than I do, but there's more to it than that." He patiently steers his boat into the backwater he knows so well and finds the best spots for catching red drum, sea trout, flounder, puppy drum, and sheepshead. Rarely does anyone walk off of his boat empty handed.

He says he caught the "fever for fishing" as a child, freshwater fishing with his father around their home in Amelia Island. It was always a passion, but it didn't pay the bills until 2006, when he quit his day job and started his own backwater fishing charter business.

Red drum, Florida's most widespread estuarine fish, are among the most caught fish on Lawrence's trips. They have rust-colored backs that fade into white bellies with a characteristic black spot at the base of the tail. They were overfished in the early and mid-1980s, Lawrence says, "but stocks are coming back up, and there are plenty for catching now." Still, the daily limit is two per person and eight total per boat, and they have to be between eighteen and twenty-seven inches long. The rules might seem confusing, but having a guide like Lawrence takes all of the guesswork out of a day on the water. "I've been fishing my whole life. It's what I live and breathe."

This is one of his favorite ways to prepare red drum (also called redfish). You can substitute any other drum in this recipe or, really, any other firm, mild fish.

LAWRENCE PIPER

1 Melt 2 tablespoons butter in a large sauté pan over medium-low heat. Add green onions and cook 4 minutes, or until softened. Add capers and olives, cooking 3 minutes more.

2 Stir in fish stock and bring to a boil over high heat. Reduce heat to medium and simmer until reduced by half, about 8 minutes.

3 Stir in cream and simmer until reduced by half, about 5 minutes. Stir in lemon juice and keep sauce warm over low heat.

4 Season fish with salt and pepper. Melt remaining 2 tablespoons butter over medium-high heat. Add fish and cook 3 minutes. Flip and cook 1 to 3 minutes longer, or until fish is just firm and cooked through.

5 Spoon sauce over fish just before serving.

4 tablespoons unsalted butter, divided

4 green onions, white and light green parts, chopped

1 tablespoon capers

½ cup chopped green olives

1¼ cups fish stock or bottled clam juice

1 cup heavy cream

2 tablespoons fresh lemon juice

2 (6-ounce) red drum fillets

Coarse salt and freshly ground black pepper, to taste

THE ST. JOHNS RIVER

FROM ITS SPONGY SOUTH FLORIDA BEGINNINGS
at its headwaters near Fort Drum to its grand
stride into the Atlantic Ocean near Jacksonville,
the St. Johns River courses with Florida heritage.
The river's entire length—40 miles of marsh
and 270 miles of open water—stretches across a
timeless landscape.

The inky ribbon, connected by a series of
lakes and smaller rivers and creeks, was a liquid
path of discovery for many, from ancient Native
Americans to intrepid explorers to new settlers.
And for a river that doesn't seem hurried from
the get-go, the St. Johns changes personality
with remarkable swiftness.

After Fort Drum, the first discernible
channels of the river rise within the marsh
south of Lake Hell 'n' Blazes. Here the St. Johns
shares a lifeline with the Kissimmee and St.
Lucie Rivers. Lily blossoms wink open at sunrise,
blizzards of dragonflies flutter between the
tufts of saw grass, and Everglade snail kites
knife through the humid air.

As the St. Johns winds north, the deep
navigable channel is a series of twists and turns
that can challenge a boater not patient enough
to watch the current. Just past where the
Econlockhatchee River joins the St. Johns is Lake

Harney, and the river's route begins to widen and
stretch out in magnificent form. The hammock
land is velveteen and the air crisp and clean.

Skirting past Lake Jesup, the current sets a
course for Lake Monroe, a wide, shallow lake
in Sanford, once a key stop for steamships
bringing goods and people to Florida's interior.
Gone suddenly are the hazy outstretches of
marsh that embrace the upper-river portions.
The waters become dark and purposeful as they
push past the shore.

At Astor, the river narrows again, seemingly
to catch its breath before it plows straight
ahead for an eleven-mile run across Lake
George, the second-largest lake in Florida, after
Lake Okeechobee.

As the river scoots past Drayton Island and
then Georgetown, its banks rise high, and the
path takes several graceful curves. Pushing on,
the waterway widens with strength at Palatka.
The final run into Jacksonville offers wonderful
vistas. As the city's skyscrapers rise up, the
river lumbers on, taking on a sophisticate's
flair for a short while. Two or three more
curves, past a mix of industrial ports and
peaceful shorelines, and the Atlantic Ocean
opens wide to receive the river.

SALT-ROASTED SHEEPSHEAD

| SERVES 2 TO 4 |

SHEEPSHEAD, A GRAY-AND-BLACK-STRIPED FISH that swims in abundance in the Atlantic, probably gets its name from its characteristic front teeth, which look curiously similar to a sheep's (or a human's, for that matter). Inside, things get even stranger: rows of dull, molar-like teeth line the inside of its mouth, which help the fish crack into various crustaceans. They may not be the prettiest fish in the sea, but they are absolutely delicious, with flaky yet firm mild flesh. Fishermen in the know go to jetties and pylons where sheepshead like to find their food. They are notorious bait thieves, so catching them requires some practice and patience, but the extra time is well worth it.

Cooking a whole fish may seem daunting, but it's actually quite easy. The salt crust keeps the fish super moist and makes it very forgiving of exact temperature and cooking time. Feel free to swap out different herbs or add to the dill. Parsley or basil would also be lovely. Our Green Olive Salsa Verde, page 232, is a delicious accompaniment to this dish.

1 lemon, thinly sliced

1 bunch fresh dill

1 whole (4- to 5-pound) sheepshead, gutted, and scaled

6 egg whites

3 cups coarse salt

TIPS FOR BUYING FRESH FISH

1 Line a rimmed baking sheet with parchment paper. Place lemon slices and dill inside cavity of fish.

2 Beat egg whites with an electric mixer in a large bowl until soft peaks form; fold in salt.

3 Place one-fourth cup salt mixture on the bottom of the prepared baking sheet, making a layer about 1 inch wider than fish.

4 Place fish on salt mixture, then spoon remaining mixture on top, packing around fish and sealing any cracks.

5 Roast fish 20 to 25 minutes, or until a paring knife inserted through crust and into fish is warm to the touch. Remove from oven and set aside 10 minutes.

6 Crack salt crust and pull it away from sides of fish. Cut away and remove top fillet from bones and transfer to a platter. Lift bones from top of remaining fillet and discard. Transfer remaining fillet to platter.

* Buy from a seafood market with high turnover and ask where the fish comes from.
* Bring a cooler with ice with you, or have fish packaged with a bag of ice to keep it as cold as possible until you get home.
* Inspect fish carefully before buying. It should smell clean, not fishy, and should be moist and shiny and have no dry edges.
* When buying whole fish, look for glossy skin and clear, full eyes; the inside of gills should be red.

BLACKENED CATFISH

| SERVES 4 |

WHEN FLORIDA NATIVE TIM CHANNELL OPENED HIS RESTAURANT on the bank of the Withlacoochee River in Dunnellon, he chose the name Stumpknockers after the small spotted sunfish that populate the river and swim among the submerged cypress knees.

An outside bar and deck offer an unspoiled view of the river canopied by lush trees. Inside, the restaurant has a warm, rustic feel and a staff that treats everyone like family. "We're a bit off the beaten path," Tim says, "but I think that's why people like to come here. They breathe in the fresh air, watch the current run, and rest assured that old Florida still exists."

When a restaurant is named after a fish, the best items on the menu should have fins. And Stumpknockers does not disappoint. Its blackened catfish is one of its most popular dishes, thanks in part to the super-fresh, clean-tasting fish.

There are many species of catfish in Florida, which can be found in both freshwater and salt water. Channel catfish (*Ictalurus punctatus*) is the most common on restaurant menus. Its meat is white, juicy, and tender and can range in flavor from strong and earthy to sweet and clean.

1 tablespoon garlic powder

1 tablespoon paprika

1 tablespoon onion powder

1 tablespoon dried thyme

1 teaspoon coarse salt

1 teaspoon smoked paprika

1 teaspoon freshly ground black pepper

1 teaspoon cayenne pepper, or more to taste

4 (6-ounce) catfish fillets

2 tablespoons peanut oil

1 Combine dry ingredients in a small, shallow bowl. Dredge both sides of catfish in seasoning mix, shaking off excess.

2 Preheat peanut oil in a large cast-iron skillet over medium-high heat. Place fish in hot skillet in batches and cook until it flakes easily with a fork, 3 to 4 minutes per side.

FLORIDA SEAFOOD BOIL

| SERVES 10 TO 12 |

4 pounds small potatoes, such as red, purple, and/or fingerlings

5 quarts water, divided

2 tablespoons cayenne pepper, or more to taste

¼ cup coarse salt

2 tablespoons black peppercorns

¼ cup mustard seeds

1 tablespoon celery seeds

1 tablespoon coriander seeds

2 sprigs fresh thyme

3 garlic cloves, minced

4 bay leaves

2 pounds kielbasa or other spicy link sausage, cut into 1½-inch pieces

6 ears corn, husked

2 cups white wine

4 spiny lobster tails

12 live blue crabs

4 pounds head-on shrimp

Cocktail sauce, for serving (see "Year-Round Sauces & Accessories" for suggestions)

Lemon wedges, for serving

Melted butter, for serving

ON COOL SPRING AFTERNOONS, we know our friends will gather at the mention of beer on ice, good music, and a steamy pot of seafood. We provide pie tins as plates and dish towels for napkins and forgo a tablecloth for a few layers of newspaper. The food is served right on the table. There's nothing fancy about a boil—it's uncomplicated, messy fun.

1 Place a steamer basket in the bottom of an extra-large stockpot. Add potatoes. Put 2½ quarts water in a large pitcher. Stir cayenne, salt, peppercorns, mustard seeds, celery seeds, and coriander seeds into water. Pour mixture into pot with remaining water.

2 Toss in thyme sprigs, garlic, and bay leaves and bring to a rolling boil; cook 5 minutes. Add sausage and corn and return to a boil. Cook until potatoes are tender, about 10 minutes.

3 Pour wine into pot. When steam rises, add lobster tails and crabs. Cover and cook 5 minutes. Add shrimp. Cover and cook until shrimp are opaque, about 3 minutes.

4 Scoop ingredients out of pot directly onto center of newspaper-lined table. Serve with lemon wedges, cocktail sauce, and melted butter.

SAUTÉED SHRIMP and FETA

| SERVES 4 |

ALONG THE ANCLOTE RIVER, less than a mile from the Gulf of Mexico, Tarpon Springs looks a bit untouched by time, with distinctive blue-and-white buildings dating back to the 1800s, sidewalk cafes, and fishing boats tethered along the waterfront. The little city, listed on the National Register of Historic Places, was named for the abundant tarpon in surrounding waters, but is best known as "the sponge capital of the world."

Turtle fishermen in 1873 discovered sea sponge beds at the mouth of the Anclote River when the sponges snagged their nets, and the sponge business soon shifted its center from Key West, Cuba, and the Bahamas to Tarpon Springs.

John Cocoris, a young Greek sponge buyer, brought hundreds of Greek immigrants, who expanded and refined the sponging industry. By 1900, the city was considered the largest sponge port in the United States, with Greek businesses established to support the community. Eventually, blight infested most of the sponge beds and red tide devastated the industry. Recovery was slow. Less than a dozen sponge boats still harvest from the Gulf of Mexico.

Today, most visitors are there for an authentic taste of the Mediterranean, and this is the sort of dish you'll find in many of the Tarpon Springs Greek eateries, a melding of the bold coastal flavors of Greece and the southern United States. Look for imported feta at your supermarket—the flavor and texture are incomparable to the domestic kind. You can swap the rice for orzo pasta, or skip the rice and serve with crusty bread.

4 tablespoons butter

1 small onion, finely diced

2 garlic cloves, finely minced

1 pound medium shrimp, peeled and deveined

1½ cups crumbled feta cheese

½ cup chopped, seeded tomatoes

½ cup dry white wine

3 tablespoons fresh lemon juice

3 tablespoons chopped fresh parsley

2 tablespoons finely chopped fresh oregano

Coarse salt and freshly ground black pepper, to taste

Cooked long-grain white rice, for serving

1 Heat butter in a large skillet over medium-high heat. Add onion and cook until golden, about 5 minutes. Add garlic and sauté 30 seconds. Add shrimp and sauté about 2 minutes, or until just pink.

2 Stir in feta, tomatoes, wine, lemon juice, parsley, and oregano and cook about 2 minutes. Season with salt and pepper. Serve hot or at room temperature with rice.

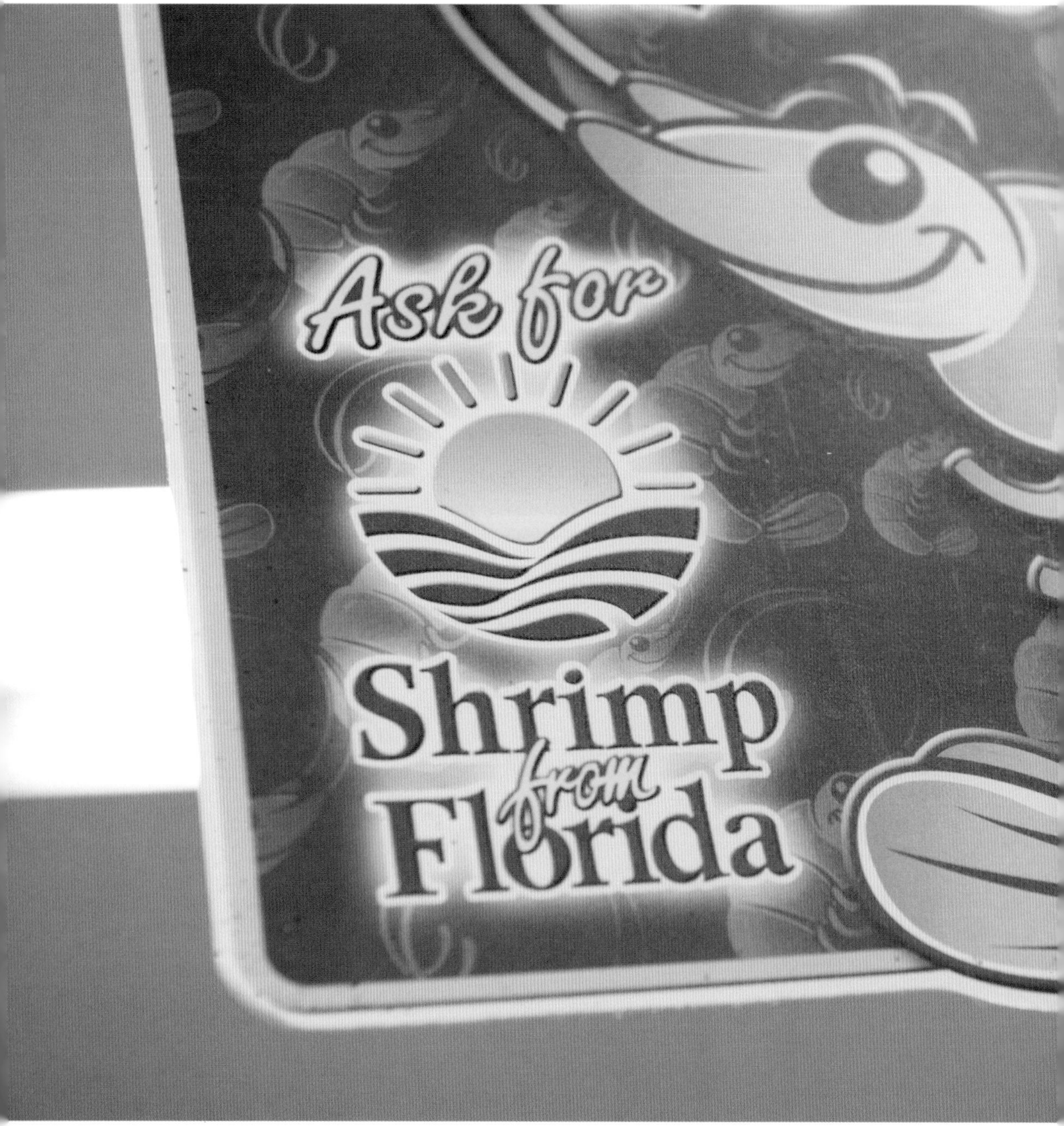
Ask for
Shrimp
from
Florida

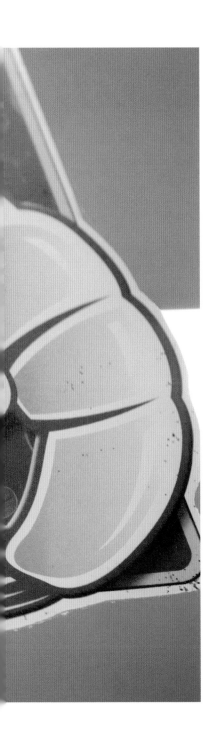

EATING SUSTAINABLE SEAFOOD

ALTHOUGH OCEANS COVER MORE THAN 70 PERCENT of the Earth, the supply of seafood isn't endless. Overfishing can damage ocean ecosystems, which are important to the health of the entire planet. Consuming sustainable seafood—that is, seafood that is plentiful and able to quickly reproduce, and that is fished and harvested in a way that doesn't harm natural habitats or other species—can make a big difference.

According to Monterey Bay Aquarium's Seafood Watch, nearly 85 percent of the world's fisheries are currently overfished or are in danger of becoming so. It can take decades for populations to recover, if at all. One of the easiest ways to know that you are eating sustainable seafood is to check the Seafood Watch program (montereybayaquarium.org), which offers a handy guide based on species population, fishing/ farming practices, health concerns, and more. There's even an app for smartphones. The recommendations are science based and peer reviewed and use ecosystem-based criteria to indicate which seafood items are "best choices" or "good alternatives" and which ones should be avoided.

America's fishing policies have improved, mostly because of the 1996 Sustainable Fisheries Act requiring regulators to define overfishing, identify fish and shellfish that are in trouble, and set target goals for rebuilding stocks.

Farm raised can be a better choice than wild caught, but not always. Because of higher standards and oversight, U.S. farm-raised fish and shellfish are better options than those from Asia.

At the supermarket, read labels and look for country of origin and whether the seafood is farm raised or wild caught. Look for logos for the Marine Stewardship Council and Friends of the Sea, which show that the seafood is certified as sustainable. And be bold enough to ask your grocer or fishmonger to buy wild caught and sustainable catches from responsible fisheries.

O'STEEN'S FAMOUS ST. AUGUSTINE FRIED SHRIMP

| SERVES 4 |

2 eggs, beaten

2 tablespoons water

3 dozen large fresh shrimp, peeled with tails intact, butterflied

1 teaspoon fine sea salt

1 cup all-purpose flour

1 cup extra-fine cracker meal

Peanut oil, for frying

JUST OUTSIDE HISTORIC DOWNTOWN ST. AUGUSTINE, O'Steen's Restaurant welcomes visitors with an illuminated sign featuring a shrimp in a top hat and tails, but there's nothing fancy about this humble North Florida eatery. Robert O'Steen, out of work due to a railroad strike, opened the diner in 1965. A month after the restaurant opened, Robert hired a twelve-year-old boy named Lonnie Pomar—in 1983, Lonnie took the reins when Robert retired.

Lonnie carries on the O'Steen's legacy today, serving made-from-scratch southern favorites. Locals and visitors line up around the building for the fried chicken, squash casserole, and deviled crab, but the most sought-after plate on the menu is the golden fried shrimp. They can serve up to 1,400 pounds of shrimp a week during the summer months, all of which comes from Florida's East Coast, and most of which comes from Northeast Florida.

Any variety of shrimp works for this recipe—use whatever is freshest. To butterfly the shrimp, cut the vein out of the top, then slowly slice until the shrimp are almost flat. O'Steen's cuts all the way through, leaving the tails intact, to create a Y shape, creating more surface area for the thin, crisp coating. You can make your own cracker meal by pulsing soda crackers in a food processor until they are very finely ground.

1 Combine eggs and water in a medium shallow dish. Set aside.

2 Sprinkle shrimp with salt, tossing to coat evenly. Dip each shrimp in flour, knocking off excess.

3 Dip shrimp into egg wash, then into cracker meal, shaking off excess.

4 Pour enough oil to reach 3 inches up the sides of a deep, heavy pot and heat over medium until it reaches 310°F on a deep-fry thermometer.

5 Working in batches, add shrimp to hot oil. Fry 2 to 3 minutes, or until shrimp are just cooked through and coating is golden. Transfer to a plate lined with a brown paper bag to drain.

CAPELLINI with LEMON and CAVIAR

| SERVES 6 TO 8 |

GENE EVANS GREW UP DIVING AND EXPLORING underwater worlds. As a kid, he never considered buying a fish tank—he built his own and always pondered how to make them bigger and better. Today, Gene is one of the state's best known aquaculture farmers and patriarch of the self-described "first family of Florida caviar." It's a ten-year-old's dream come true—to grow up and make a living from your boyhood hobby.

On 1,700 remote acres east of Pierson, he is monitoring large tanks teeming with osetra, sevruga, and beluga sturgeon. Sturgeon are docile, primitive-looking creatures that look like an unfortunate cross between a catfish and a shark. The fish, which are more associated with the cold waters of the Caspian Sea, are known for their white meat and prized roe.

According to the Department of Agriculture and Consumer Services, in early 2009, the Evans Fish Farm became the first in this hemisphere to spawn a sturgeon from egg to egg. And its Anastasia Gold caviar is turning heads at top industry tastings.

Mote Marine Laboratory in Sarasota also has a sturgeon operation, although it is a different variety of fish, and the nonprofit corporation is aimed at research and education more than commercial ventures. In the fall of 2006, Mote became the first organization in the state of Florida to harvest caviar grown at Mote Aquaculture Park, and chefs in top-notch restaurants are now actively sourcing Florida caviar for menus.

Checking the tanks with his dog Blu—short for Beluga—Gene reflected on the future of his operation: "We send millions of dollars out of this country to purchase caviar. I'd like to see that stay right here. We're on the right path and we are hitting benchmarks that no one thought we would. If you believe in something, you have to be prepared to ride it out."

Though we usually prefer to enjoy caviar dolloped on blini with a touch of crème fraîche, this decadent pasta is also incredibly luxurious and a great way to stretch a small container of caviar to serve several people. Store the leftover roe in the jar, turning over every few days to ensure that it's evenly coated in oil.

1 Cook pasta in boiling salted water according to package directions. Drain and toss with butter in a warm serving bowl.

2 Stir in crème fraîche. Toss again, very gently, with 6 tablespoons caviar. Season to taste with salt and pepper. Top with lemon zest, fresh dill, and remaining caviar. Serve immediately.

1 pound angel hair pasta

2 tablespoons unsalted butter

8 ounces crème fraîche, at room temperature

8 tablespoons sturgeon caviar, divided

Coarse salt and freshly ground black pepper, to taste

Freshly grated lemon zest, for garnish

Fresh dill sprigs, for garnish

SWEET CORN HUSH PUPPIES with GUAVA JELLY

SERVES 8

PEOPLE WILL TELL YOU THEY STOP at Deal's Famous Oyster House in Perry for the plump shellfish, mullet, grouper, and warm hushpuppies served with guava jelly. And that's certainly part of the draw. But we would wager most visitors settle into one of the red booths in hopes that owner Zodie Horton will break out the pogo stick and play some music. Yes, pogo stick.

With the fervor of a full-on southern revival, Zodie will announce: "Everybody got good nerves?" Sometimes musicians drop by to accompany her peculiar percussion on their guitars. Sometimes she simply turns on a toe-tapping recording of "Cotton-Eyed Joe." Stripped of its jumping mechanism, the pogo stick is fixed with a wobbly cymbal on top and another cymbal and a tambourine midway down the pole. Using a drumstick, Zodie beats a staccato rhythm with the contraption as she moves around the room. Some nights, customers join in with tambourines while others clap along. As Zodie moves the stick from table to table, the rubber tip on the bottom makes a low rumbling noise as it's dragged across the worn wood floor.

There's magic in that stick. Within minutes of its rattling and awkward clanging filling the room, spirits lift and smiles widen. Welcome to the Church of Southern Hospitality. "The finest people in the world come through that door," says Zodie, greeting a large group of regulars. She places the pogo stick against the wall, grabs some menus, and seats the guests at a large table.

In her book *Cross Creek Cookery*, Florida writer Marjorie Kinnan Rawlings wrote: "Fresh-caught fried fish without hush puppies are as man without woman, a beautiful woman without kindness, law without policemen." At Deal's, warm hushpuppies are served with guava jelly on the side. This mix of sweet and savory is a wonderful match.

1 Pour oil to a depth of 3 inches in a Dutch oven or deep cast-iron skillet and heat to 375°F, or until a drop of batter bubbles in the hot liquid.

2 Combine cornmeal, flour, onion, corn, and sugar. Add egg and buttermilk and stir just until moistened. Let stand 10 minutes.

3 Working in 3 batches, drop batter by rounded tablespoons into hot oil and fry until golden, 2 to 3 minutes on each side.

4 Drain on paper towels and serve warm with guava jelly.

Vegetable oil for frying

1½ cups self-rising yellow cornmeal mix

¾ cup self-rising flour

½ cup diced sweet onion

¾ cup sweet corn kernels

1½ tablespoons sugar

1 large egg, lightly beaten

1¼ cups buttermilk

Guava jelly, for serving

MINT COLESLAW

| SERVES 8 TO 10 |

THIS COOLING SIDE SALAD of pale green cabbage, sweet peas, and fresh mint will take the heat out of summer meals. If using fresh peas, lightly steam in the pod, drain, let come to room temperature, chill, then remove peas from pod. When we take this slaw to picnics or on the boat, we use frozen peas straight from the freezer. By the time we're ready to eat, the peas have thawed and the slaw is still nice and cool. If you want a more pronounced mint flavor, add a drop of mint extract to the mayonnaise mixture.

1 cup mayonnaise

1 tablespoon superfine sugar

5 cups thinly sliced fresh green cabbage

2 cups fresh or frozen sweet peas

¼ cup fresh mint leaves, washed and very thinly sliced

Combine mayonnaise and sugar and blend well. Combine cabbage, peas, and mint in a large bowl. Fold in dressing to coat completely.

FLORIDA BEAN CAVIAR

| SERVES 8 TO 10 |

AFTER THE MIXTURE HAS MARINATED OVERNIGHT, we like to pour it into a small colander set over a bowl to catch all of the flavorful juices. The vinegary onion- and celery-seasoned liquid makes an easy and tasty marinade for shrimp or fish.

2 (15-ounce) cans black-eyed peas, drained and rinsed

¾ cup canola oil

½ cup red wine vinegar

½ cup finely chopped celery

½ cup finely chopped red onion

Coarse salt and freshly ground black pepper, to taste

3 garlic cloves, crushed

Liberal dash hot sauce

1 Put black-eyed peas in a large bowl. Whisk remaining ingredients to combine in another large bowl. Pour over black-eyed peas, stirring gently to combine.

2 Refrigerate overnight or longer, stirring twice a day. Serve cold.

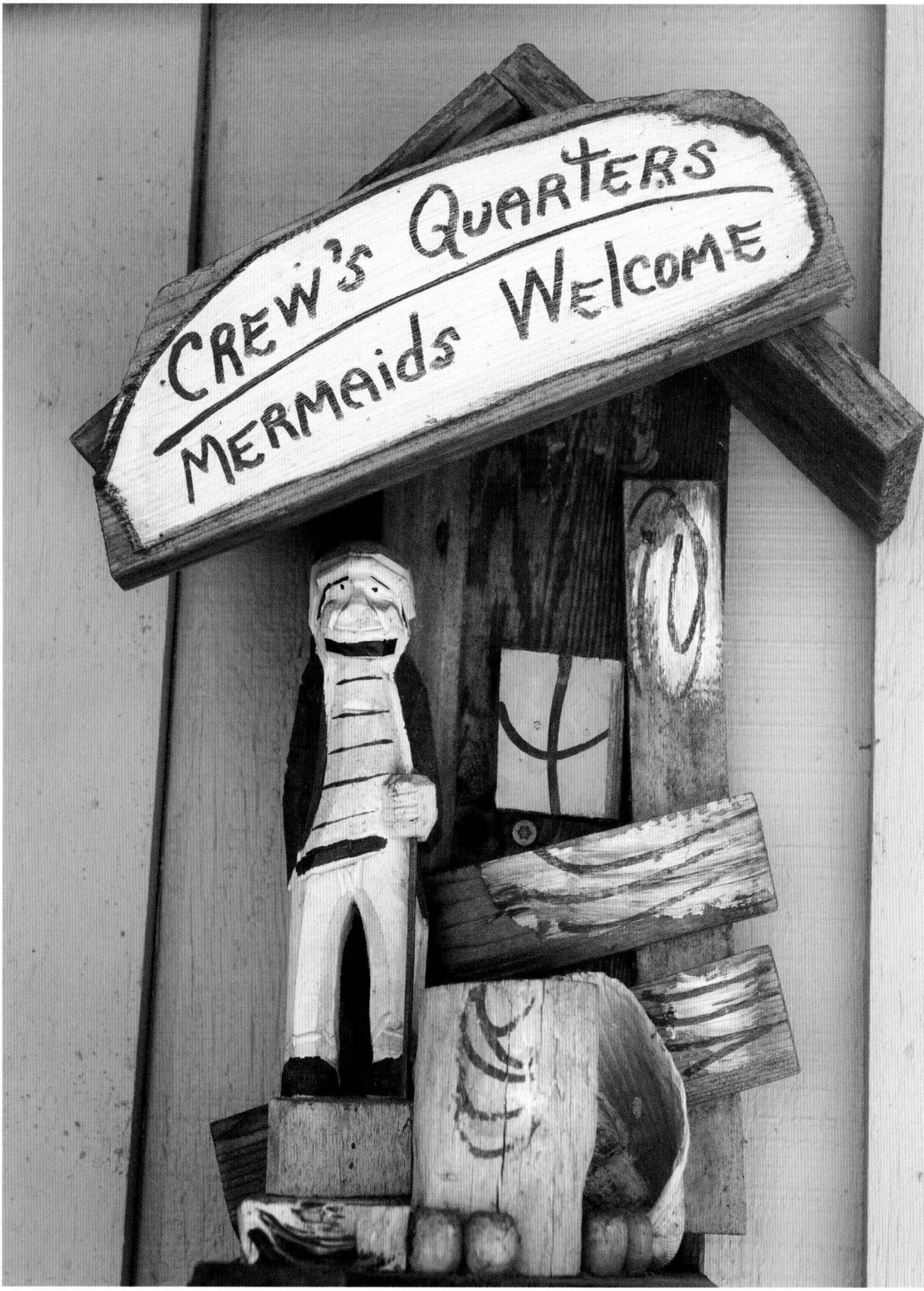
CREW'S QUARTERS
MERMAIDS WELCOME

CARROT and ZUCCHINI PAKORAS

| SERVES 12 |

PAKORAS ARE INDIAN FRIED VEGETABLE FRITTERS that usually include two or three ingredients, such as vegetables, fish, rice, cheese, or meat. Ours include veggies that can usually be found year-round in Florida farmers' markets. We love them alongside a seafood meal for a play on traditional hushpuppies. They freeze well, so even if you're having a small dinner, make the whole batch.

1 Blanch carrots, zucchini, and potato in salted boiling water for 1 minute. Drain in a colander for 10 minutes, then transfer to paper towels to cool and dry completely.

2 Combine grated vegetables, onion, parsley, thyme, garlic, garam masala, hot sauce, eggs, salt, and pepper in a large bowl. Stir in flour a little at a time. Mixture should loosely cling together without forming a stiff batter. Sprinkle batter with cornmeal, if using, and stir to blend. If needed to keep batter loose, add water 1 tablespoon at a time.

3 Heat a shallow pool of oil in a cast-iron skillet to 375°F. Working in batches, scoop heaping tablespoons of batter into the hot oil. Fry until fritters are golden, 2 to 3 minutes per side. Drain on paper towels and serve immediately or keep warm in the oven until ready to serve.

2 small carrots, washed and grated

1 small zucchini, washed and grated

1 Yukon gold potato, washed and grated

¼ cup chopped sweet onion

½ cup chopped fresh parsley

1 tablespoon fresh thyme leaves

1 garlic clove, minced

1 teaspoon garam masala, or to taste

Hot sauce, to taste

2 large eggs, beaten

Coarse salt and freshly ground black pepper, to taste

1¼ cups chickpea flour or all-purpose flour

1 tablespoon fine yellow cornmeal, optional

Water as needed

Vegetable oil for frying

SPICY CUKE and PEANUT SALAD

| SERVES 4 |

2 seedless cucumbers, diced

1 green serrano chile, minced (remove seeds for less heat)

Juice of 1 lemon

1 teaspoon agave nectar

¼ teaspoon cayenne pepper

½ cup roasted, salted peanuts

1 tablespoon peanut, canola, or walnut oil

1 teaspoon mustard seeds

Coarse salt, to taste

THIS IS A CREATION OF OUR FRIEND ANNE-MARIE DENICOLE, who is one of the most creative cooks we know. You can make this salad in 10 minutes as you grill some fish, or stir the ingredients into plain Greek yogurt and serve on the side for a play on a cooling Indian raita.

1 Combine cucumbers, chile, lemon juice, agave nectar, and cayenne in a medium bowl. Pulse peanuts in a food processor until they are very finely chopped and add to cucumber mixture.

2 Heat oil in a nonstick skillet over high heat. When oil begins to shimmer and smoke, carefully add mustard seeds, covering skillet with a spatter screen or lid. When seeds stop popping, pour hot oil and seeds over salad, stirring gently to combine.

3 Taste for salt, sweetness, and lemon, adjusting as necessary. Serve cold or at room temperature.

BEST BLUEBERRY COBBLER

| SERVES 8 TO 10 |

MARCH THROUGH MAY IS THE HEIGHT of Florida blueberry season, when you'll find the little blue fruit in abundance. And while blueberries are delicious fresh, there's nothing like a crispy-topped cobbler bubbling hot from the oven and crowned with a scoop of vanilla-bean ice cream. There are countless riffs on classic cobbler, but this super-easy, foolproof version is one of our favorites. You can reheat leftovers, but it's also delicious straight from the fridge.

2 cups all-purpose flour

2 cups sugar, plus more for sprinkling on fruit

2 sticks unsalted butter, melted

6 cups fresh blueberries

1 Preheat oven to 350°F. Combine flour and sugar. Add butter and stir until mixture is soft and crumbly. Set aside.

2 Put blueberries in a 13 x 9 x 2-inch baking dish; lightly sprinkle with sugar if berries are tart. Cover with topping. Bake for 50 minutes, or until top is golden and just starting to brown and sides are bubbling. Remove from oven and cool slightly before serving.

CHOCOLATE CAKE with SALTED CARAMEL ICING

| MAKES 1 (9-INCH) LAYER CAKE |

CHOCOLATE CAKE

2 cups sugar

1¾ cups all-purpose flour

¾ cup baking cocoa

1½ teaspoons baking soda

1½ teaspoons baking powder

1 teaspoon salt

1 cup milk

½ cup vegetable oil

2 eggs

2 teaspoons vanilla extract

1 cup boiling water

SALTED CARAMEL FROSTING

1 cup sugar

3 tablespoons water

¼ cup unsalted butter

½ cup half and half or cream

1 teaspoon sea salt

½ cup shortening or softened unsalted butter

3 to 4 cups powdered sugar

Coarse sea salt

THIS LAYER CAKE IS THE PERFECT ENDING for a seafood boil. The golden caramel frosting has a flourish of sea salt that reminds us of our connection to the ocean and that really makes the flavors sing. Juliet and Olivia Welsh, the teenage twins of Pam's neighbor Kellie, created this masterpiece. If thirteen-year-olds can bake a cake from scratch, so can you.

MAKE CAKE

1 Preheat oven to 350°F. Grease and flour two 9-inch round baking pans.

2 Stir together sugar, flour, baking cocoa, baking soda, baking powder, and salt in the bowl of a stand mixer. Add milk, oil, eggs, and vanilla and beat at medium speed for 2 minutes, scraping bowl occasionally. Stir in boiling water.

3 Divide batter equally between pans. Bake for 30 to 35 minutes, or until a tester inserted in the center comes out clean. Cool 10 minutes, then remove cake from pans to wire rack to cool completely.

MAKE FROSTING AND ASSEMBLE CAKE

1 Mix sugar and water in a saucepan over low heat. Stir constantly as sugar dissolves and comes to a boil. Increase heat to medium and boil uncovered, without stirring, until sugar turns golden brown, 5 to 7 minutes. Remove from heat and add butter and half and half. (The caramel will foam up and steam.) Add sea salt and whisk vigorously until caramel begins to thicken. Cool to room temperature.

2 Transfer caramel to a large mixing bowl. Add shortening or softened butter and beat on medium speed until light and fluffy. Gradually add powdered sugar, beating on medium speed, until icing is spreadable.

3 Spoon about one-third of salted caramel frosting onto center of bottom layer and spread with a knife or offset spatula to cover evenly. Place second layer on top of frosting and spread one-third of frosting over it. Spread sides with remaining frosting. Sprinkle generously with sea salt.

Summer's
HEAT

CRAB · SCALLOPS · SQUID · FLOUNDER · GROUPER · POMPANO · AMBERJACK · BUTTER BEANS · ZU

RMELON • CLAMS • BLUE CRAB • SCALLOPS • SQUID • FLOUNDER • GROUPER • POMPANO • AMBERJA

PAPA DOBLE

| MAKES 1 DRINK |

1 cup crushed ice

2 ounces white rum

½–1 ounce fresh lime juice

½ ounce fresh grapefruit juice

¼ ounce maraschino liqueur

THE PAPA DOBLE WAS ERNEST HEMINGWAY'S made-to-order daiquiri created at one of his favorite Havana, Cuba, haunts, El Floridita bar. An avid adventurer and fisherman, he once described the look of the drink as "like the sea where the wave falls away from the bow of a ship when she is doing thirty knots."

It's quite sour, so if you like drinks without a lot of pucker, add simple syrup to taste (to make simple syrup, combine equal parts sugar and water in a pan and cook until sugar dissolves). It should be noted that maraschino liqueur is quite different from maraschino cherry juice. It's clear and dry and made from the fruit and pits of sour marasca cherries.

Fill a blender one-quarter full with crushed ice. Add remaining ingredients and blend on high until the mixture is frothy. Serve immediately.

ERNEST HEMINGWAY

BILL McCOY

RUMRUNNER

| MAKES 1 DRINK |

ONE OF CENTRAL FLORIDA'S MOST COLORFUL Prohibition-era characters was Bill McCoy, a nondrinking rumrunner who lived in Holly Hill. He was famous—or infamous, depending on which side of the bar you were standing. The Halifax Historical Museum has described Bill, who was an accomplished boat builder and captain, as "six feet two, shoulders like a cargo hatch, slim waist, a voice like a fog horn, lean tanned face, and steady eyes in a weather beaten face from long gazing over glittering waters."

Bill's exploits have been chronicled by Ken Burns in his documentary series *Prohibition*. The film credits Bill with pioneering the rum-running trade by sailing a schooner loaded with 1,500 cases of liquor from Nassau in the Bahamas to Savannah, Georgia, and pocketing $15,000 in profits from just one trip. By the end of his career, Bill claimed to have landed more than 170,000 cases of liquor during his bootlegging days.

Of his time as a rumrunner, Bill recalled: "There was all the kick of gambling and the thrill of sport, and, besides, these, there were the open sea and the boom of the wind against full sails, dawn coming out of the ocean, and nights under the rocking stars. These caught and held me most of all." Bill died at age seventy-one aboard his boat, the Blue Lagoon, in Stuart, on December 30, 1948.

Today, several Florida distillers are making artisan rums. They include Wicked Dolphin from Cape Spirits in Cape Coral and Siesta Key rum from Drum Circle Distilling in Sarasota.

Florida lore credits the Holiday Isle Tiki Bar in Islamorada with inventing the rumrunner. The libation was supposedly created out of necessity when the bar had an excess of rum and liqueurs that needed to be moved before the arrival of more inventory. Whatever the origin, it's the perfect libation for toasting a Florida sunset.

1 ounce light rum

½ ounce blackberry brandy

½ ounce crème de banana

3 ounces fresh orange juice

3 ounces pineapple juice

Dash cherry juice

½ ounce black cherry rum

Maraschino cherry for garnish

1 Combine light rum, brandy, crème de banana, and fruit juices. Shake and strain over ice.

2 Top with one-half ounce black cherry rum and garnish with a cherry.

BEER MARGARITAS

THIS IS ONE OF KATIE'S FAVORITE BEACH DRINKS, and it goes perfectly with our fried shrimp (page 38). It's OK to let the mixture steep at least 3 to 4 hours, though it's best when it sits for 12 or more. And while any light-colored beer is technically fine, we really like Mexican suds for this, like Dos Equis lager or Pacífico if you can find it.

4 teaspoons lime zest

¾ cup fresh lime juice

2 teaspoons orange zest

¼ cup fresh orange juice

¼ cup superfine sugar

Pinch coarse salt, plus additional for rimming glasses

1 cup tequila

2 (12-ounce) bottles lager beer

1 lime, cut into wedges

1 Combine lime zest, lime juice, orange zest, orange juice, sugar, and salt in a large jar. Stir until sugar dissolves. Seal jar and refrigerate overnight.

2 Strain mixture through a fine-mesh sieve into a pitcher and discard zest. Stir in tequila. Add beer, stirring gently to combine.

3 Run a lime wedge around the rim of each glass, then dip the rim into coarse salt. Fill glasses with ice and pour margaritas over. Serve with lime wedge.

CLAMS in BEER and BUTTER

| SERVES 2 |

½ stick unsalted butter

1 small sweet onion, diced

2 cups light-colored beer

1 tablespoon chopped flat-leaf parsley

¼ teaspoon coarsely cracked black pepper

3 dozen clams, well scrubbed

Crusty bread, for serving

FLORIDA CLAMS COME IN SEVERAL SIZES—the smallest are pasta necks, which have 18 to 25 per pound. For this recipe, we prefer littleneck, which have 10 to 13 per pound, or middleneck, which come 7 to 9 per pound. Clams should smell like the sea, and the shells should be free of cracks. Store live clams in a container with the lid open slightly, because they need air circulation to breathe, and discard any clams that don't open when tapped lightly.

1 Melt butter in a large pot over medium heat. Add onion and sauté until tender but not browned, about 3 minutes.

2 Pour in beer and stir in parsley and pepper. Add clams, cover pot, and bring to a boil. Cook until clams open, 4 to 5 minutes.

3 Serve clams in broth with crusty bread for dipping.

BOB'S CONCH FRITTERS

| MAKES 3 DOZEN |

CONCH FRITTERS ARE A FLORIDA KEYS CLASSIC. While queen conch no longer are fished in Florida waters, the large sea snails remain a part of the culture of the Conch Republic (the nickname for Key West), and every fan recommends a different roadside eatery that serves their favorite version of the deep-fried fritters. Fortunately, conch still is plentiful in the Turks and Caicos Islands in the Caribbean, and the meat can be found frozen in U.S. seafood markets.

This recipe is from fourth-generation Floridian Bob Morris, best known as the author of the Zack Chasteen mysteries, set in Florida and the Caribbean. At his book launches, you'll often find Bob tending a pot of super-hot oil filled with crispy, golden fritters floating to the surface. "In most conch fritters you can't taste the conch," says Bob. "That's because the fools who make them buy ground conch instead of whole conch and don't want to go to all the trouble of pounding it themselves." These fritters have chunky pieces of sweet conch so you know for sure what you are eating. Add a rumrunner (page 65) and you've got a party.

Use a meat mallet or the side of a heavy rolling pin to pound the conch, ensuring it will be tender and not chewy. »

Opposite page:
BOB MORRIS

CONCH FRITTERS

2 cups conch meat (about 1 pound)

Juice of 1 lime

Generous amount hot sauce

2 cups self-rising flour

2 eggs, beaten

1 onion, finely diced

1 green pepper, finely diced

2 teaspoons paprika

Coarse salt and freshly ground black pepper, to taste

½ cup milk

Peanut oil, for frying

DIPPING SAUCE

1 cup ketchup

2 tablespoons fresh lime juice

Hot sauce, to taste (Bob prefers Minorcan datil pepper sauce if you can find it)

Freshly ground black pepper, to taste

1 tablespoon mayonnaise

MAKE DIPPING SAUCE

1 Mix ketchup, lime juice, hot sauce, and pepper in a bowl.

2 Whisk mayonnaise with a fork in a separate small bowl until creamy, then combine with ketchup mixture. Refrigerate until ready to serve.

MAKE FRITTERS

1 Pound conch on a cutting board until the thick membrane breaks and conch is tender and scaloppini-thin. Slice into bite-sized chunks.

2 Squeeze lime over conch in a large bowl. Stir in hot sauce; set aside to marinate for a few minutes.

3 Mix flour, eggs, onion, green pepper, paprika, salt, and pepper into conch. Batter will be stiff; add just enough milk to hold it together.

4 Heat about 2 inches of peanut oil in a cast-iron skillet to 350°F. Drop tablespoon-sized balls of batter into hot oil and cook about 4 minutes, stirring occasionally, until golden brown and they float to the surface. Remove from skillet and drain on paper towels.

5 Serve hot with dipping sauce.

JOE PATTI'S HOT CRAB DIP

| SERVES 10 |

1 pound blue crab meat

1 pound cream cheese, softened

1 bunch green onions, green tops and bulbs, finely chopped

½ cup mayonnaise

1 teaspoon Worcestershire sauce

2 dashes hot sauce

½ cup sliced almonds, lightly toasted

Crackers, pita chips, or toast points, for serving

IN THE EARLY 1930S, ANNA AND JOE PATTI started selling fish from their front porch on DeVilliers Street in Pensacola. Captain Joe developed a reputation for being hard to please—he refused much more fish and shellfish than he accepted. From the 1960s through the early 1990s, Joe Patti's served all of the restaurants along the Gulf Coast of Florida and Alabama.

Eventually, the business emphasis changed to retail, and, in the late 1990s, the store expanded, with a gourmet delicatessen, sushi bar, and wine shop. Gourmet crab dips are one of the store's best sellers. Joe Patti's is open 361 days a year, and family members are still an integral part of the operation.

In a pinch, you can make this dip with refrigerated crabmeat, but it's really best with fresh. This is the perfect use for an excess of crabmeat after a particularly successful day of crabbing. In the market, colossal lump or jumbo lump is the highest grade and the most expensive. Lump crabmeat consists of broken jumbo and large chunks of body meat. Back-fin grade is made up of smaller broken chunks of lump meat mixed in with flakes of white body meat. You can use a mixture of all grades in this super-rich dip.

1 Heat oven to 350°F.

2 Blend crab, cream cheese, green onions, mayonnaise, and Worcestershire sauce in the bowl of an electric mixer. Scrape down sides of bowl and stir in hot sauce.

3 Spray a 1-quart glass baking dish with nonstick spray. Spoon crab mixture into dish and spread almonds over the top. Bake until edges are bubbly, 20 to 30 minutes. Serve with crackers, pita chips, or toast points.

LAKE OKEECHOBEE

CLEARLY VISIBLE TO ASTRONAUTS in outer space, Lake Okeechobee is a whopping 730 square miles but exceptionally shallow, with an average depth of just nine feet. Named by the Seminoles, Okeechobee means "big water" in the Seminole Indian language—*oki* (water) and *chubi* (big). You can't see shore to shore on Florida's "inland sea," once saline, now freshwater as rainfall has replenished it over time.

Anglers often refer to Lake Okeechobee as the "bass fishing capital of the world," but it is also known for exceptional bluegill and speckled perch fishing. "And there's also turtle, gator, frog legs, catfish, and shellcracker for good eating," says Captain Michael Shellen,

who has been one of the top bass fishing guides on Lake Okeechobee since 1979. Captain Mike has his own favorite fishing holes with names like the Monkey Box, Moonshine Bay, Fisheating Creek, Hay Fields, and the Cow Pasture. "You can expect to tangle with a 7- to 10-pound bass," says Captain Mike. "The lake record is 15 pounds 5 ounces."

Captain Mike strongly promotes a catch-and-release policy for all bass caught in Lake Okeechobee, but you won't have to tell tales about the one that got away; he'll gladly help you create a custom trophy fish mount for bragging rights.

Opposite page:
MARK *and* **KATHRYN LEE**

GRILLED SHRIMP PO' BOYS with PINK SAUCE

| SERVES 4 |

4 tablespoons unsalted butter

2 large garlic cloves, finely minced

½ teaspoon plus ¼ teaspoon coarse salt, divided

3 heaping tablespoons mayonnaise

1 tablespoon apple cider vinegar

1 teaspoon prepared horseradish

½ cup ketchup

1 teaspoon mustard

Pinch sugar

1 pound jumbo shrimp, peeled and deveined

Olive oil, for brushing

1 large French baguette, sliced almost in half horizontally and cut into 4 equal pieces

2 cups shredded romaine lettuce

IN FLORIDA, YOU CAN FIND FRESH SHRIMP in various shades of white, brown, pink, and even red. Really, any wild-caught shrimp from Florida makes a great po' boy, but the sweet, firm pink shrimp from the Gulf, often called Key West pinks, are our favorite for this recipe. The shrimp are caught in the Gulf of Mexico, where the coral-tinged sand gives them their characteristic hue. And because they live in areas of water less populated by other fish, the lack of bycatch (nontarget species that get caught in shrimp nets) makes them an especially eco-friendly choice, as well.

The magic in this recipe is in the pink sauce, which is so versatile. Katie's friend Joanna Wallace shared her family recipe, which likely started with her great-grandmother, whom everyone called Dammy. Joanna adds extra horseradish and vinegar, while her mom, Priscilla Eubanks, makes it a little creamier with extra mayo. It's great as a dip for boiled shrimp, as a topping for crab cakes, and with Aunt Glo's Fried Green Tomatoes (page 219). We call for jumbo shrimp because they're easier to grill.

1 Combine butter, garlic, and half-teaspoon salt in a small saucepan over medium-low heat. Cook until butter melts and garlic is very fragrant, about 5 minutes. Pour into a large bowl and set aside.

2 Combine mayonnaise, vinegar, horseradish, ketchup, mustard, one-fourth teaspoon salt, and sugar in a medium bowl. Cover and refrigerate until ready to use.

3 Preheat a grill to medium-high. Thread shrimp onto metal skewers and brush with oil. Grill until shrimp just turn pink and are opaque, about 1 to 2 minutes per side. Immediately transfer hot shrimp to bowl with butter-garlic mixture, tossing to combine.

4 Spread both sides of baguette with pink sauce. Place a small handful of shredded lettuce on each baguette, then divide shrimp evenly among baguettes. Serve extra sauce on the side for drizzling.

HOW TO SELECT FRESH SHELLFISH IN THE SEAFOOD MARKET

* Buy lobsters and crabs alive whenever possible and choose the liveliest ones in the tank.
* Buy clams and oysters that are kept on ice, not submerged in water.
* Examine your purchase carefully. Shrimp should never feel slimy or smell like anything but saltwater. Preshucked oysters should be stored in clear liquid. Clam and oyster shells should be free from cracks and should close when tapped lightly.

GARLIC CRABS

| SERVES 4 |

IT'S QUITE A HAUL JUST FOR SEAFOOD, BUT WHEN THE PILE OF GARLIC-LADEN BLUE CRABS WAS DELIVERED TO OUR TABLE, WE KNEW IT WAS WORTH THE DRIVE.

PECK'S OLD PORT COVE IS EXACTLY 9.3 MILES OFF U.S. HIGHWAY 19 on North Ozello Trail in Crystal River. The paved path snakes along a flat plain of switchbacks, and just when you begin to think your navigation system has failed you, there it is: a large blue-gray wood building with a yacht club vibe from the exterior. Outside, a large deck welcomes guests to dine at the water's edge in an area the locals call the Ozello Keys, a marshy hammock that fades into the Gulf of Mexico.

Shallow saltwater tanks on the outdoor deck house the live blue crabs that the restaurant serves. The tanks keep the crabs lively until the kitchen needs them to fill orders. The restaurant has its own crab traps set out in the surrounding waterways, and fresh crabs are delivered throughout the week. Peck's other specialties include shrimp, scallops, seasonal fresh fish, and clam chowder. But one look around the inside dining room and outdoor deck, and you'll see most guests come for the crabs.

The kitchen staff quarters the crabs and cracks their shells, making it easy to extract the meat. A shell cracker and small forks are supplied to save your fingers from a sharp, sticky torment. You can eat until you are exhausted and as permeated with garlic as the crabs, and you will still likely have leftovers to take home.

As we sat down to eat, we heard the low rumble of approaching airboats. Owner Tommy Williams and his son Dan pulled their airboats right onto the adjoining lawn and hopped out, dogs in tow. The father-son owners are justifiably proud of their family business. "People call us from the airport when they land in Tampa or Orlando and ask how late we're open," Tommy says. "And we have customers who drive here from Daytona Beach on a weekly basis." It's quite a haul just for seafood, but when the pile of garlic-laden blue crabs was delivered to our table, we knew it was worth the drive.

Blue crabs are so named for their cobalt and orange claws, which can be as vivid as a sunset over the Gulf. Their Latin name, *Callinectes sapidus*, means "savory beautiful swimmer." Though some of our neighbors to the north are known for their blue crab, the truth is, many of the crabs served around the United States come from brackish waterways in Florida.

1 Combine vinegar, beer, salt, garlic, and seafood seasoning in a small pitcher or bowl with a spout.

2 Place a low steamer basket in the bottom of a large stockpot over medium heat. Add 1 cup water. Add half the crabs and pour in half the beer and vinegar mixture when water begins to steam. Add remaining crabs and top with remaining beer and vinegar mixture.

3 Cover pot, lower heat to simmer, and let crabs steam 20 to 25 minutes. Toss with pan liquid before serving in large bowls.

1 cup white wine vinegar

1 cup dark beer

1 tablespoon coarse salt

2 to 4 large garlic cloves, minced, or more to taste

1 tablespoon seafood seasoning, such as Old Bay

1 cup water

1 dozen live blue crabs

PASTA with SCALLOPS and SQUID

| SERVES 4 |

FOR THE SCALLOPING FAITHFUL, THE FIRST WEEK OF JULY is always reserved for opening weekend of the season. They flock to small towns with funny names like Homosassa and Steinhatchee (STEEN hatch-ee) to snorkel the shallow surrounding estuaries and pluck the brown-and-white shells from the slinky sea grass. Open only to recreational harvest, the small, tasty bivalves are easy to catch by hand—it's more Easter egg hunt than skillful fishing. Though scallops can be found all along the West Coast of Florida, populations are large enough for harvest only north of Tampa, and the official recreational harvest area spans from Hernando County north to the west bank of Mexico Beach.

Florida's Big Bend area, the geographic curve on the West Coast, is the area richest with scallops. In towns like Crystal River, Homosassa, and Steinhatchee, it's easy to find a charter boat with a knowledgeable captain at the helm during scalloping season. Outfitted with just a snorkel, mask, and fins, you can skim the grass for the well-camouflaged shells or look for the distinctive tiny bright blue eyes that peek out when the shells open slightly. It's kind of addicting, like a treasure hunt game—the more you find, the better you become at spotting the next one. (There are limits, but they're generous: two gallons of in-shell scallops per person.) When you return, on almost every dock, you'll find locals waiting with shucking knives ready to fill a bag with your sweet scallops for just a few bucks.

For this recipe, if you can't find orecchiette, you can substitute another short-cut pasta like campanelle or gemelli. Reserving and using the starchy cooking water from the pasta will both help thin the sauce and help it stick to the pasta. Keep an eye on the scallops and squid as they cook—they can overcook and turn rubbery really quickly. As soon as they are just turning opaque, they're done.

1 Bring a large pot of salted water to a boil. Fill a medium bowl with ice and cold water; set aside.

2 Cut an X in top of tomato and place in boiling water 1 minute. Remove tomato and place into ice water. Cover boiling water, remove from heat, and set aside.

3 When tomato is cool enough to handle, remove and discard skin. Core tomato and cut into bite-sized pieces, reserving juices; place tomato and juices in a medium bowl and set aside.

4 Melt 4 tablespoons butter in a large sauté pan over medium heat. Add shallots and cook until tender, 2 to 3 minutes. Add lemon juice and wine and simmer 2 minutes, or until slightly reduced.

5 Add reserved tomato and juices; break up tomato using the back of a spoon. Simmer 3 minutes, or until sauce thickens slightly.

6 Bring pot of water back to a boil, add pasta, and cook according to package directions until al dente.

7 Meanwhile, add squid and scallops to tomato mixture, tossing to coat. Cook until seafood is just opaque, about 3 minutes. Stir in remaining 2 tablespoons butter and lemon zest. Add salt and pepper to taste.

8 Reserve one-fourth cup pasta cooking water; drain pasta. Add pasta and 2 tablespoons cooking water to sauté pan, tossing to coat. Add more water if needed to thin sauce. Serve immediately.

1 medium tomato

6 tablespoons unsalted butter, divided

2 shallots, thinly sliced

1 small Meyer lemon, zested and juiced

¾ cup dry white wine (such as chardonnay)

1 pound dried orecchiette pasta

1 pound fresh Florida squid

1 pound fresh Florida bay scallops

Coarse salt and freshly ground black pepper, to taste

FLOUNDER with BROWN BUTTER and HERB SALAD

| SERVES 4 |

FLOUNDER IS A FLAT, ROUND FISH with both eyes on the same side of its head. Its fin encircles almost its whole body and ripples as the fish skims the muddy bottoms of brackish estuaries and near the sandy seashore of the Gulf of Mexico and in the Atlantic. The meat is pure white, clean, and very easy to debone when cooked. Its flavor is so mild that nutty brown butter and fresh herbs suit this fish perfectly.

2 green onions, tough tops and root ends discarded

2 large sprigs fresh dill

2 large sprigs fresh parsley

¼ cup caper berries, halved

1 teaspoon lemon zest

1 teaspoon plus 1 tablespoon extra-virgin olive oil

4 (6-ounce) ½-inch-thick flounder fillets

2 tablespoons instant flour, such as Wondra

Coarse salt and freshly ground black pepper, to taste

4 tablespoons unsalted butter

2 tablespoons fresh lemon juice

1 Quarter green onions lengthwise, then cut each quarter in half again lengthwise, creating long, slender curls. Place in a large bowl. Separate tender dill fronds from center stem and place in same bowl (discard center stem). Remove parsley leaves and very tender stems from center stem and add to bowl (discard center stem). Add caper berries, lemon zest, and 1 teaspoon oil, tossing to combine. Set herb salad aside.

2 Pat flounder with paper towels to dry thoroughly. Sprinkle with flour, brushing to fully but very lightly coat each fillet; shake off excess. Sprinkle each with a pinch of salt and pepper.

3 Heat remaining 1 tablespoon oil in a large skillet over medium-high heat until it shimmers. Add flounder, searing about 2 minutes, or until you can slide a thin spatula underneath fillets. (If the fish won't budge, give it 30 seconds and try again.) Flip fish and cook 1 to 2 minutes more, until fish just feels firm. Transfer fish to a plate and loosely tent with foil.

4 Add butter to pan, swirling to melt. Cook 1½ minutes, or until butter turns golden brown and smells nutty. Add lemon juice and remove from heat.

5 Place each flounder fillet on a serving plate. Evenly divide brown butter sauce among fillets. Evenly divide herb salad among fillets and serve immediately.

FRIED GROUPER SANDWICHES with HERBED TARTAR SAUCE

| SERVES 4 |

1 cup mayonnaise

1 tablespoon minced green onion, white and light green parts only

1 tablespoon finely chopped dill pickles

1 teaspoon chopped fresh mint

1 teaspoon chopped fresh dill

1 teaspoon chopped capers

Vegetable oil, for frying

1¼ cups all-purpose flour, divided

½ cup cornstarch, divided

1 teaspoon baking powder

1 teaspoon seasoned salt

1½ to 2 cups club soda

4 (6-ounce) fresh grouper fillets

4 sandwich buns

Bibb lettuce leaves, for serving

WHEN KATIE WAS A CHILD, SHE WOULD OFTEN ACCOMPANY her grandparents Howard and Mary Parks on their deep-sea fishing excursions off the shore of Ormond Beach. She was always so proud to help reel in the iridescent wild fish and to sit on top of the jumbo cooler that held the larger-than-she-was catches. She realizes now that there was likely a latch to keep the giant fish contained in the cooler, but her sense of responsibility was part of the fun.

The next day, her grandmother would pick up the fish from the dock, by then neatly filleted and packaged. Most of it went into the freezer, but Mary always kept out a few pieces of grouper to fry and sandwich between soft white buns with iceberg lettuce and plenty of homemade tartar sauce. This is still Katie's favorite way to eat flaky, buttery white grouper (or any white fish, for that matter).

There are more than twenty varieties of grouper found in the Gulf and Atlantic around Florida, and you can use any of them for this sandwich. Really, any firm white fish is fine here—mahi mahi or snapper would also work. The herbed tartar sauce can also be used as a dip for fried shrimp or thinned out with a little buttermilk and used as a dressing for slaw.

1 Place mayonnaise in a medium bowl. Stir in green onion, pickles, mint, dill, and capers. Cover and refrigerate until ready to serve.

2 Pour oil to a depth of 3 inches in a large, heavy-bottomed pot over medium heat. Heat oil to 375°F.

3 Meanwhile, set aside one-fourth cup flour and one-fourth cup cornstarch in a shallow dish, stirring to combine. Whisk together remaining flour and cornstarch, baking powder, and seasoned salt in a large bowl.

Add club soda until texture resembles pancake batter.

4 Dredge fish fillets in flour-cornstarch mixture, tapping off excess. Working in batches of 2, dip fillets in batter, then carefully lower into oil. Fry 2 to 4 minutes per side, until golden brown. Transfer to a plate lined with paper towels.

5 Spread a thin layer of tartar sauce on top and bottom of each bun. Place a piece of fish on bottom half of bun, then top with lettuce and top half of bun.

VIETNAMESE-STYLE ROASTED WHOLE POMPANO

| SERVES 2 |

POMPANO, PRETTY LITTLE SILVER-AND-CHARTREUSE FISH that glimmer in sunlight, are a Florida specialty—the majority of commercially harvested pompano comes from the Gulf of Mexico and the Atlantic in the Sunshine State. The pompano population rebounds quickly, so though it was once overfished, it's now considered a sustainable choice. Its meat is pleasantly oily, which gives it a rich but still mild flavor. Filleted, pompano can be expensive, so we prefer to buy the whole fish at a much friendlier price and roast it whole. Unless you are well versed on how to do it yourself, just ask your fishmonger to clean the fish for you.

2 (1- to 1½-pound) pompano, scaled and gutted

2 stalks fresh lemongrass, cut in half lengthwise

1 large bunch fresh cilantro

1 small bunch Thai basil

2 teaspoons plus 1 tablespoon peanut oil

½ cup crushed roasted peanuts

¼ cup chopped green onions

2 tablespoons chopped fresh mint

2 tablespoons fresh lime juice

2 teaspoons fish sauce

½ teaspoon sugar

1 Preheat oven to 475°F.

2 Stuff cavity of each fish with 2 lemongrass stalk halves, about 8 stems of cilantro, and 4 stems of basil, reserving remaining cilantro and basil. Drizzle 2 teaspoons oil on the bottom of a small baking sheet and place fish on top. Drizzle remaining tablespoon oil over fish.

3 Roast until fish is cooked through, 15 to 18 minutes.

4 Meanwhile, roughly chop enough remaining cilantro to make 2 tablespoons. Repeat with remaining basil. Combine peanuts, green onions, chopped cilantro, basil, mint, lime juice, fish sauce, and sugar in a medium bowl. Stir to combine.

5 Remove fish from oven and make a cut near the head and another near the tail. Lift and remove top fillet and discard bones. Repeat with bottom fillet. Serve with herb-peanut mixture.

DESSIE PRESCOTT'S DEVILED CRABS

| SERVES 10 |

IN 1995, HEATHER SET OFF in search of the soul of a favorite author, Marjorie Kinnan Rawlings, and along the way, she met Marjorie's muse, Dessie Prescott. Dessie was born August 4, 1906, in Island Grove, a hamlet in Alachua County. She started hunting when she was just five years old, charging through the scrub to gather birds the grownups had shot. "My uncle said even at the age of five or seven that I was the best bird dog, the best retriever he ever owned. And why I never got bit by a rattlesnake, I'll never know," she once told Heather.

Heather and a college friend, Dr. Leslie Kemp Poole, came to know Dessie after they decided to re-create a chapter of Marjorie Kinnan Rawlings's *Cross Creek*. The chapter, "Hyacinth Drift," is a long recounting in luxuriant detail of a ten-day boat trip that took Marjorie and Dessie out into the St. Johns River near Fort Christmas through to the Ocklawaha River at Eureka. With Dessie piloting the boat, the two women cut a path through some of Florida's most beautiful, untamed waterways.

To prepare for their trip, Heather and Leslie spent several weekends at Dessie's home, which sat along a backwash stretch on the Withlacoochee River. As Dessie looked over their charts, she served up advice for the boat trip: "Don't let anyone talk you out of it."

In "Hyacinth Drift," Marjorie describes Dessie as an astonishing woman. "She was born and raised in rural Florida, and guns and campfires and fishing-rods and creeks are corpuscular in her blood. She lives a sophisticate's life among worldly people. At the slightest excuse she steps out of civilization, naked and relieved, as I should step out of a soiled chemise. She is ten years my junior, but she calls me, with much tenderness, pitying my incapabilities, 'Young un.'"

Later in life, Dessie operated the Withlacoochee River Lodge off U.S. Highway 19 in Citrus County, a rustic haven for outdoor enthusiasts from all over the country. A fair amount of the fishermen would arrive at the

> SHE WAS BORN AND RAISED IN RURAL FLORIDA, AND GUNS AND CAMPFIRES AND FISHING-RODS AND CREEKS ARE CORPUSCULAR IN HER BLOOD.

camp and assume she was the wife of the owner or just an employee. "It was a man's world then," Dessie would say. "I'd laugh and tell them, 'You can stay and catch lots of fish or you can go home. It doesn't matter to me.'" The ones that stayed were overwhelmed by the fish they caught and the insights of the queen of Florida's frontier scrub.

Dessie remained vigorous into her early nineties. "The world is my oyster, and I spent my life cracking it," she would tell her friends. She died of cancer in 2002 at the age of ninety-five at her home.

Dessie Prescott wasn't tied to rules, recipes, or road maps. Once she told Heather how much she liked deviled crab. When asked how she made hers, Dessie said "fresh blue crab, eggs, and whatever I have on hand." To prepare the crab shell for stuffing and baking, remove legs and open up the underside with kitchen shears. If you don't want to go to the trouble, you can bake the mixture in individual gratin dishes.

6 large eggs

1½ cups chopped green onions, white and light green parts

¼ cup chopped fresh celery leaves

1 tablespoon Worcestershire sauce

⅓ cup fresh lemon juice

¼ teaspoon freshly ground nutmeg

1 tablespoon fresh lemon zest

1 tablespoon fresh lime zest

1 pound fresh blue crabmeat, drained (save cleaned shells for baking crab)

1½ cups unsalted butter, melted and divided

5 cups soft breadcrumbs, divided

1 cup chopped fresh parsley

½ teaspoon coarse salt

¼ teaspoon freshly ground pepper

Hot sauce, to taste

1 Heat oven to 400°F.

2 Combine eggs, green onions, celery leaves, Worcestershire sauce, lemon juice, nutmeg, zests, and crabmeat in a large bowl.

3 Gently fold in 1 cup melted butter, 4 cups breadcrumbs, parsley, salt, pepper, and hot sauce with a rubber spatula.

4 Spoon crabmeat mixture into 10 baking shells or individual baking dishes, such as small ramekins. Divide remaining 1 cup breadcrumbs and remaining half cup melted butter evenly among baking dishes.

5 Bake, uncovered, 20 minutes, or until thoroughly heated. Turn oven setting to broil and broil 1 to 2 minutes, or until golden brown. Serve immediately.

BECKYJACK'S FISH TACOS

| SERVES 2 |

NOT FAR FROM WEEKI WACHEE SPRINGS, where "mermaids" have delighted visitors since 1947, sits BeckyJack's Food Shack. The humble roadside eatery on Cortez Boulevard abounds with a sense of place and warmth, every inch of the walls covered with signs, quotes, photos, and kitschy nautical-themed décor. In 2009, Kim Curtis and Joe Foster took over the establishment, which had been operated for decades by the late Becky De La Rosa.

They were planning to name their restaurant to reflect Joe's love of burgers, but after discovering a sign out front with Becky's name on it, and still lamenting the death of their former boss, Jack Newkirk, the name BeckyJack's was born. "We felt good karma from both names to guide us through," Kim says. "Becky had this place for more than thirty years, and Jack was such a dear friend and mentor."

Kim and Joe developed a from-scratch menu and quickly gained a local following. "Food doesn't have to be expensive to taste good," says Kim. "We use fresh ingredients and treat all of our customers like friends. And they are." A lot of people come for the smilin' Bob's smoked fish dip, the juicy burgers, the crab patties, or to have Kim and Joe cook a fresh catch. But the fried crunchy fish tacos are a favorite. The texture comes from rolling and coating fish fillets in a thick batter of cornflakes and lightly toasted almonds.

As word has spread, BeckyJack's no longer belongs to the locals. "We are amazed at how many people drive up from Tampa or over from Orlando," Kim says. Becky and Jack would have been proud.

Kim uses swai, but any sweet white fish will work in this recipe, such as amberjack, a medium-firm fish, which is found throughout the Gulf of Mexico from near-shore waters out to depths of 300 feet and occasionally deeper.

1 Place flour in a shallow dish and season with salt and pepper. Combine cornflakes and almonds on a rimmed plate, crushing slightly, but leaving the texture mostly intact. Pour beaten eggs and milk into another shallow bowl and stir to combine.

2 Coat each fillet in flour, then in eggs. Dredge the fillets in the cornflakes and nut mixture, coating well. Let fish rest 5 minutes.

3 In a large cast-iron skillet heat oil to 350°F. Carefully lower one fillet at a time into oil and fry until golden brown. Set fish on paper towels to allow excess oil to drain off. Slice into strips.

4 Smear some tartar sauce in each tortilla, add the fish and lettuce, and serve with salsa.

1 cup all-purpose flour

Coarse salt and pepper, to taste

1 cup cornflakes

1 cup sliced almonds, slightly toasted

3 to 4 large eggs, beaten

4 tablespoons whole milk

2 (8-ounce) amberjack fillets

Oil for frying

6 (6-inch) flour tortillas

Tartar sauce, to taste

Chopped iceberg lettuce

Salsa for serving

FLORIDA SUCCOTASH

| SERVES 4 |

2 cups fresh butter beans

¼ pound fresh chorizo sausage, casing removed

1 garlic clove, finely minced

2 small zucchini, diced

2 cups fresh corn kernels

4 green onions, root ends and dark green tops removed

½ teaspoon coarse salt

¼ teaspoon freshly ground black pepper

LOOK FOR FRESH BUTTER BEANS AT LOCAL FARMERS' MARKETS in the spring and summertime. If you can't find any, you can use frozen, but it's really worth it to seek out the fresh ones. Fresh chorizo is raw, unlike the hard, cured variety. It's usually sold near the breakfast sausages in the supermarket.

1 Cook butter beans in a large pot of salted water until just tender, 20 to 30 minutes; drain and set aside.

2 Heat a large sauté pan over medium-high. Add chorizo and cook until golden, breaking up into small pieces, about 4 minutes. Add garlic, stirring to combine. Cook until fragrant, about 30 seconds.

3 Add zucchini, cook 2 minutes, then stir in butter beans, corn, and green onions. Season with salt and pepper. Cook just until everything is heated through, about 2 minutes more.

CHARRED CORN with SPICY LIME BUTTER »

| SERVES 4 |

4 ears corn, shucked

Light olive oil, for grilling

4 tablespoons unsalted butter

1 lime, zested and juiced

1 serrano chile, seeded and minced

2 tablespoons chopped fresh cilantro

Coarse salt, to taste

CORN IS A NO-BRAINER DURING THE SUMMERTIME. Even though we call for grilling this corn, you can achieve similar results by placing it under the broiler for a few minutes.

1 Preheat an outdoor grill to medium-high. Brush corn lightly with oil and grill, turning often, until tender and charred, 6 to 8 minutes.

2 Meanwhile, combine butter, lime zest, 2 teaspoons lime juice, and chile in a small saucepan over medium heat. Cook 3 minutes, then remove from heat and set aside.

3 Cut corn off cob while still hot. Place in a large bowl and toss with butter mixture. Stir in cilantro and salt to taste.

GRILLED ROMAINE with MISO-LEMON DRESSING

| SERVES 4 |

QUICKLY GRILLING THE ROMAINE ON ONE SIDE lends a touch of smoky flavor but allows the lettuce to retain its crunch. You can use a stovetop grill pan if the afternoon heat or summer rain prevent you from grilling outdoors.

1 Pulse bread in a food processor until it forms medium crumbs. Melt butter in a large skillet over medium-high heat. Add breadcrumbs and stir to fully coat. Toast, stirring constantly, until breadcrumbs are crisp and golden brown, about 5 minutes. Set aside.

2 Whisk together lemon zest, lemon juice, and miso paste in a medium bowl. Slowly stream in one-fourth cup oil, whisking constantly, until completely combined. Add more oil to taste, if desired. Set dressing aside.

3 Preheat a grill to medium-high.

4 Remove any wilted outer leaves from romaine hearts. Cut a thin slice off of root ends, then cut each heart in half lengthwise, keeping root ends intact. Brush with oil and season with salt and pepper.

5 Place romaine cut side down on grill and cook just until slightly wilted and grill marks appear, about 3 minutes.

6 Cut roots off and discard. Transfer lettuce to a platter and top with tomatoes. Drizzle with dressing and sprinkle with breadcrumbs.

2 cups cubed French bread

2 tablespoons unsalted butter

1 lemon, zested and juiced

1 tablespoon light miso paste

¼ to ⅓ cup light olive oil, plus additional for brushing

2 small romaine hearts

Coarse salt and freshly ground black pepper, to taste

2 heirloom tomatoes, cut into wedges

GRILLED PEACHES with RICOTTA SALATA and WATERCRESS

SERVES 4

4 small Florida peaches, pitted and sliced into quarters

Olive oil, for brushing

Coarse salt, to taste

4 cups (loosely packed) watercress, tough stems removed

2 tablespoons white balsamic vinegar

2 tablespoons roasted walnut oil

8 thin slices ricotta salata

Coarsely cracked black pepper

THIS SALAD CAME ABOUT ONE NIGHT when Katie had already grilled some shrimp for the Grilled Shrimp Po' Boys (page 80) and wanted to utilize the still-glowing coals. She glanced around the kitchen, saw some peaches, and tossed them on the grill. You can swap the watercress for another tender green (arugula would work well), and if you can't find ricotta salata, you can use good imported feta. But don't skip the walnut oil. Its rich nuttiness elevates this dish to something really savory and flavorful.

1 Preheat an outdoor grill or indoor grill pan to medium-high. Brush peaches with oil and sprinkle with salt. Grill peaches 2 minutes per side, until lightly charred. Set aside.

2 Toss watercress with vinegar and oil in a large bowl. Season with salt to taste. To serve, mound watercress in the center of a serving plate. Arrange peaches around watercress and top with ricotta salata. Sprinkle with pepper.

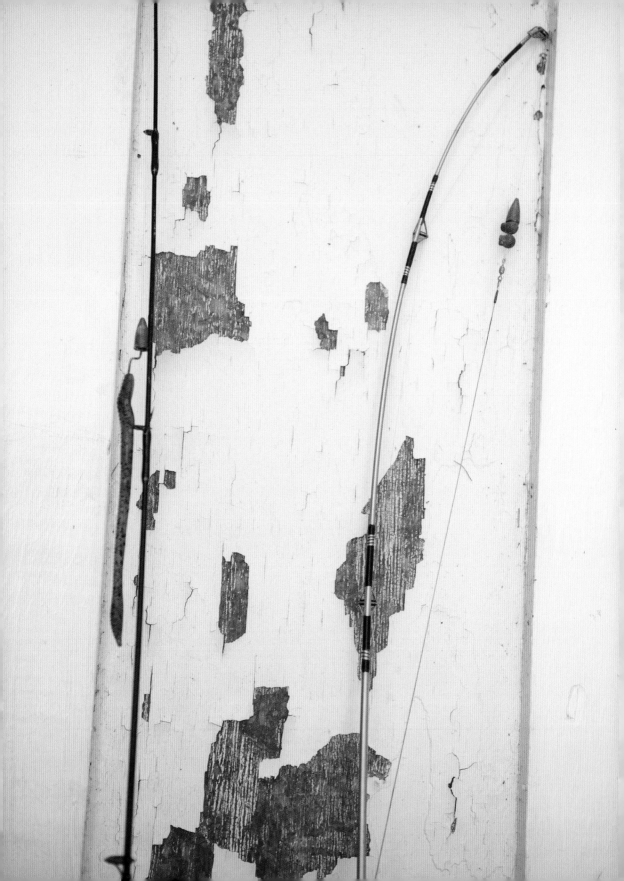

WATERMELON GRANITA
with BASIL-MASCARPONE CREAM

| SERVES 4 TO 6 |

½ cup heavy cream

⅓ cup (loosely packed) chopped fresh basil

4 cups cubed seedless watermelon

1 tablespoon fresh lime juice

¼ to ⅓ cup plus 2 tablespoons sugar

⅓ cup mascarpone cheese

THIS IS OUR HOMEMADE VERSION OF GELATI—layered Italian ice and ice cream. Depending on the sweetness of your watermelon, you may not even need a quarter cup of sugar. Add a bit at a time until it tastes just sweet enough to be dessert.

1 Combine cream and basil in a small saucepan over medium heat. Bring cream just to a bare simmer, then immediately remove pan from heat. Pour mixture into a heatproof bowl. Set aside to cool to room temperature, then refrigerate 3 hours.

2 Purée watermelon and lime juice in a blender. Add sugar to taste, then blend again.

3 Pour mixture into a 13 x 9 x 2-inch metal baking pan. Freeze 1 hour, then scrape sides and edges, mixing ice crystals into center. Return to freezer 1 hour, then repeat scraping process. Freeze 2 hours, or until firm. Scrape mixture with a fork to form fluffy flakes. Cover and freeze until ready to serve.

4 Pour basil cream through a fine-mesh sieve; discard basil. Combine cream, mascarpone, and remaining 2 tablespoons sugar in a large bowl, stirring until mixture is smooth. Whip mixture until soft peaks form.

5 Spoon granita into serving dishes and top with a bit of basil-mascarpone cream. Add a second layer of granita and top with another dollop of cream. Serve immediately.

BLACK-BOTTOM CUPCAKES

| MAKES 1 DOZEN |

WE'RE CRAZY ABOUT THESE "ICING-ON-THE-INSIDE" CUPCAKES, perfect for packing for a boat trip or picnic. Our pal Karen McClintock borrowed this retro recipe, a rich spin on classic devil's food cake with a gooey cheesecake center, from her mother-in-law. These little black-and-white treats are sinfully delicious hot, cold, or at room temperature. You can make them ahead; they'll keep in an airtight container for 2 to 3 days. (They actually taste better the second day.)

8 ounces cream cheese, at room temperature

1 egg

1⅓ cups sugar, divided

½ teaspoon salt, plus a pinch, divided

1 (6-ounce) package semisweet chocolate chips

1½ cups all-purpose flour

¼ cup baking cocoa

1 teaspoon baking soda

1 cup water

⅓ cup vegetable oil

1 tablespoon apple cider vinegar

1 teaspoon vanilla extract

1 cup chopped nuts, optional

1 Combine cream cheese, egg, one-third cup sugar, and a pinch of salt. Beat with an electric mixer until smooth. Stir in chocolate chips and set aside.

2 Preheat oven to 350°F. Line 12-cup muffin tins with paper or foil baking cups.

3 Stir together remaining 1 cup sugar, flour, cocoa, baking soda, and remaining one-half teaspoon salt in a large bowl. Add water, vegetable oil, vinegar, and vanilla, stirring until smooth.

4 Fill baking cups one-third full, then top with 1 tablespoon of cream cheese mixture. Sprinkle with chopped nuts, if desired.

5 Bake 30 minutes, or until the cupcakes feel springy to the touch (a tester inserted in the chocolate part will come out clean). Be careful not to overbake.

6 Turn out onto a rack to cool. Cupcakes can be stored at room temperature for up to 3 days in an airtight container.

Fall's

SEASON OF PLENTY

WHITING • SWORDFISH • LOBSTER • MAHI MAHI • SNOOK • AVOCADOS • OKRA • LIMES • RED SN

NG • SWORDFISH • LOBSTER • MAHI MAHI • SNOOK • AVOCADOS • OKRA • LIMES • RED SNAPPER •

ATLANTIC SEA BREEZE COCKTAIL

⟦ MAKES 1 DRINK ⟧

THE SEA BREEZE COCKTAIL has been a bar menu favorite since the 1920s—even when Prohibition kept it behind closed doors. The drink is part of a family of "breezes," including the bay breeze (swap grapefruit juice with pineapple) and the cape codder, which has no grapefruit juice.

Combine vodka and juices and stir until combined. Pour into a tall glass filled half full with crushed ice. Garnish with lime wedge and mint sprig.

1½ ounces vodka, chilled

½ cup cranberry juice, chilled

2 tablespoons fresh grapefruit juice, chilled

Crushed ice

1 lime wedge

1 sprig fresh mint

BOATHOUSE PUNCH

⟦ SERVES 20 ⟧

THERE ARE MANY VARIATIONS OF THIS POTENT LIBATION found at waterside restaurants throughout Florida. This recipe is inspired by Harry T's Lighthouse in Destin and the lounge at the Conch House Marina Resort in St. Augustine.

1 Place sugar and peels in the bottom of a punch bowl. Using a muddler or wooden spoon, mash ingredients together. Let stand 1 hour.

2 Gently stir in lemon juice, orange juice, mango juice, bourbon, and brewed tea.

3 Add sparkling wine just before serving. Serve over crushed ice with orange slices and freshly grated nutmeg.

1 cup extra-fine sugar

Colored peels and juice of 3 lemons

Colored peels and juice of 1 large orange

1 cup bottled mango juice

1 quart bourbon

1 quart freshly brewed strong green or white tea, cooled

1 (750-ml) bottle dry sparkling rosé

Crushed ice

Orange slices, for garnish

Freshly grated nutmeg, for garnish

MINORCAN CLAM CHOWDER

| SERVES 6 |

"FRIENDS DON'T LET FRIENDS EAT IMPORTED SHRIMP," reads a bumper sticker on the window outside Singleton's Seafood Shack in the village of Mayport, just up the road from Jacksonville Beach. It's a fitting sentiment for this restaurant situated on the last bit of St. John's River before it meets the Atlantic. In 1969, Ray and Ann Singleton sold breakfast and lunch to the crews of the shrimp boats that would dock nearby. That turned into dinner service as well, and the restaurant grew over the years (literally—the Singletons built their restaurant over pilings into the St. Johns). Today, shrimp boats draped with lines and pulleys and nets and other fishing vessels still dock on each side of the restaurant. Ray and Ann's son, Dean, is now at the helm of the pleasantly unrefined seafood shack.

A fancy restaurant this is not—the sign is hand painted, the ceilings are low, the wood floors creak, and everything is served on Styrofoam. One annex houses a makeshift museum of model boats, and nautical tchotchkes line the walls and shelves everywhere you look. Singleton's may be a total dive, but the seafood is fresh, cooked simply, and done well—fried, broiled, and blackened are the most popular preparations. A huge metal cooler full of ice inside the front door holds steel bowls with the daily fresh catches, from sheepshead and flounder to triggerfish and jumbo shrimp.

One of the most popular items on the menu, Minorcan clam chowder, draws from the culture of some of Northeast Florida's first residents, immigrants from Minorca, an island off the coast of Spain. (Dean is a ninth-generation Minorcan.) The brothy, spicy chowder is reminiscent of Manhattan clam chowder, but has a bigger bite and a floral flavor that comes from the addition of a regional specialty, datil peppers. This is our take.

In the restaurant, they freeze the fresh clams in their shells overnight, which helps save the clam liquor and makes them easier to shuck and chop. Chowder clams are the largest you can buy; if you can't find them, just buy the largest ones available. Datil peppers can be hard to come by outside of Florida. Substitute with a small habanero chile for similar flavor and bite.

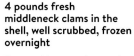

1 Shuck and roughly chop clams; reserve in a bowl with liquor and set aside.

2 Heat a stockpot over medium heat; add bacon and cook until golden and beginning to crisp, 5 to 8 minutes. Add onion, bell pepper, celery, and datil pepper, stirring to combine. Cook until onion softens, about 5 minutes. Add garlic, cooking 1 minute more. Stir in potato and lemon juice.

3 Add clam juice, crushed tomatoes, and Worcestershire sauce. Stir well to combine. Cover and turn heat to high. Bring to a boil, then immediately lower heat to medium-low. Simmer until flavors blend, about 30 minutes. Add clams and reserved liquor, stirring to combine. Cook 5 minutes more.

4 pounds fresh middleneck clams in the shell, well scrubbed, frozen overnight

½ pound bacon, chopped

½ large sweet onion, diced

½ green bell pepper, seeded and diced

½ small celery stalk, diced

1 datil pepper, stemmed, seeded, and finely chopped

2 large or 4 small garlic cloves, minced

1 small russet potato, peeled and diced

1 tablespoon fresh lemon juice

1 cup bottled clam juice

1 (28-ounce) can crushed tomatoes

1 teaspoon Worcestershire sauce

RED SNAPPER CEVICHE

| SERVES 4 |

RED SNAPPER IS CURRENTLY VERY HEAVILY AND STRICTLY regulated in Florida, with low allowances, which is a controversial topic for many fishermen and fisheries, most of which want looser regulations. Debate aside, red snapper is highly prized for its sweet, nutty flavor. Because of its scarcity, sometimes other fish are sold as red snapper. To be sure you're getting real red snapper, look for its characteristic bright red irises. Don't let the snapper marinate more than 3 hours before serving, or it will become mushy.

1 Place snapper in a large glass or stainless steel bowl. Add salt, tossing to coat well. Add lime juice, grapefruit juice, and olive oil and toss to combine. Stir in chile and green onion. Cover and refrigerate 40 minutes, gently stirring every 10 minutes.

2 Just before serving, stir in avocado and cucumber and sprinkle with cilantro. Serve with plantain chips.

½ pound fresh boneless, skinless red snapper fillets, diced

¼ teaspoon coarse salt, plus additional to taste

½ cup fresh lime juice

¼ cup fresh grapefruit juice

2 tablespoons extra-virgin olive oil

1 small fresh hot chile, such as habanero or datil, seeded and finely diced

1 green onion, white and light green parts only, thinly sliced

1 avocado, diced

½ cucumber, peeled, seeded, and finely diced

¼ cup roughly chopped fresh cilantro leaves

Plantain chips, for serving

CORTEZ BOTTARGA BREAD SALAD with BUTTER BEANS and CAPER VINAIGRETTE

| SERVES 2 |

> "IT'S ALWAYS
> BEEN ABOUT
> SUPPORTING
> HIS HOME
> COMMUNITY AND
> SPREADING THE
> BOTTARGA LOVE."

ANNA MARIA FISH CO. FOUNDER SETH CRIPE grew up in the small fishing village of Cortez. His family was in the local restaurant industry, and many of his friends were avid fishermen, but Seth's passion was wine. He moved to California when he was seventeen to learn about winemaking. Years later, while dining at Thomas Keller's illustrious French Laundry in Yountville, California, he tasted bottarga for the first time. Bottarga, the salted and dried roe sack of a female mullet, is firm, rust-colored, and packed with rich, briny umami flavor. It's most often used as a condiment—grated over pasta, pizza, and salads—and is used around the world, in countries such as France, China, Taiwan, and Greece.

Seth was staggered to learn that this highly prized culinary item came from mullet, considered by many to be a "trash" fish, and one that swims in abundant supply in the waters surrounding his hometown. "Seth figured, why not make it there, instead of shipping the roe halfway around the world?" says Jaclyn Bloch, marketing manager for Anna Maria Fish Co.

Inspired, Seth traveled to Europe to learn the process of making bottarga. He then returned to Florida, worked with researchers at the University of Florida to perfect the technique, then set up shop in Cortez, where he brines, salts, and air-dries the roe sacks for three weeks. He sent samples to high-profile chefs, who were impressed with the flavor and quality of the domestic product. Cortez Bottarga—the first and only U.S.-made bottarga—is now featured on menus in restaurants around the country.

Seth works directly with fishermen who catch mullet and pays them above-average wages. His goal has always been to bring income and recognition to the historic village where he grew up, says Jaclyn. "It's always been about supporting his home community and spreading the bottarga love."

Seth's bread salad recipe is a salty, nutty combination that lets the singular flavor of the bottarga really shine. If you don't have a mandoline, or V-slicer, for the celery, just use your sharpest knife to slice it as thinly as possible.

1 Place capers in a deep bowl, add a sprinkle of salt, and mash using a pestle or the back of a spoon. Add lemon juice, parsley, and champagne vinegar. Stir to combine. Slowly whisk in 6 tablespoons olive oil.

2 Preheat oven to 400°F. Cut bread into 1-inch cubes and arrange in a single layer on a baking sheet. Bake for about 10 minutes.

3 Heat 2 tablespoons oil in a large sauté pan over medium heat. Add beans and cook, without stirring, 5 minutes. Add a sprinkle of salt and pepper and toss gently. Cook 5 minutes more, until golden brown. Remove beans from pan.

4 Add remaining 2 tablespoons oil to pan and return to medium heat. Add toasted bread, tossing to coat in oil, and cook until golden, about 3 minutes.

5 Combine bread and beans in a large bowl. Add celery and arugula; slowly drizzle on caper vinaigrette. Top with bottarga just before serving.

2 tablespoons capers, rinsed

Sea salt, to taste

1 tablespoon fresh lemon juice

2 tablespoons Italian parsley, chopped

2 tablespoons champagne vinegar

10 tablespoons extra-virgin olive oil, divided

½ (16-ounce) loaf crusty bread

1 (14-ounce) can Italian butter beans, drained and rinsed

Freshly ground black pepper, to taste

1 cup very thinly sliced celery

Handful of arugula, washed and torn into bite-sized pieces

2 tablespoons grated Cortez Bottarga

BUFFALO-STYLE FLORIDA FROG LEGS

| SERVES 4 |

BLAKE RAWLINS HAS BEEN GIGGING FOR FROGS in the dark waters of Lake Woodruff near DeLeon Springs since he was a teenager and taught himself to watch for the shining eyes and white chest of a big, bellowing bullfrog. Now in his thirties, he still loves a night in the warm moonlight to putter just off the shoreline in his airboat, stalking the amphibians, a sport that lies somewhere between hunting and fishing.

Gigging is nearly a lost art in Florida, a simple sport that involves nothing more than a boat, a pole with a sharp gig on the end for spearing the catch, and good hand-eye coordination. Frog legs, the only part worth eating, are a Florida cracker delicacy, the sweet, tender meat soaked in milk, lightly coated in flour, and fried.

Blake wears a headlamp to spy the frogs, which sit on the eel grass, lily pads, and coontail with their heads just above water. They are frozen in place by the bright light. "We idle on the airboat and get pretty close, our twelve-foot gig poles just about six inches from the frog," says Rawlins. Speed and dexterity count: they quickly pierce just behind the frog's head with the gig, or sometimes just grab the frog with their hands.

On a good night, Blake and his buddies gig 200 frogs, but they can score up to 500 if they stay out past midnight, he says. He hunts bullfrogs from March through September and freezes the legs for big, happy fish frys that the Rawlins family hosts in cool winter months in the hammock at Highland Park Fish Camp in DeLand. "Since I was about five years old, we've been frying up frog legs, bass, speck, even deer meat," he says. "There's nothing like sharing your catch with family and friends."

The Rawlins family has been guiding anglers on Florida waters at Highland Park Fish Camp for more than three generations. "My granddad, Derris 'Dink' Rawlins, started the camp in 1962, and now my father, Ron, and my Uncle Rick run the place," Blake says.

And as much as he loves fishing for bass and speckled perch, Blake is a serious frog leg aficionado. "If I was on death row," he says, "I'd ask for frog legs for my last meal."

We love this zippy version of fried frog legs from Orlando Chef Jamie McFadden of Cuisiniers, served with spicy Buffalo sauce, blue cheese sauce for dipping, and a side of pickled celery. The treatment enhances the sweet white meat, which has a flavor that's very similar to that of chicken. »

"IF I WAS ON DEATH ROW," HE SAYS, "I'D ASK FOR FROG LEGS FOR MY LAST MEAL."

PICKLED CELERY

1 bunch celery, including leaves

4 large sprigs fresh dill

1 cup apple cider vinegar

1 cup water

3 tablespoons sugar

1 tablespoon salt

2 teaspoons mustard seeds

2 teaspoons ground coriander

1 teaspoon peppercorns

BLUE CHEESE DIPPING SAUCE

1 cup crumbled blue cheese

2 tablespoons buttermilk

1 cup mayonnaise

½ cup chopped green onions, white part only

1 tablespoon Worcestershire sauce

1 tablespoon red wine vinegar

1 teaspoon chopped garlic

1 teaspoon minced shallots

Coarse salt and freshly ground black pepper, to taste

MAKE THE PICKLED CELERY:

1 Slice celery into ¼-inch-thick slices and place in a clean 1-quart jar with dill and celery leaves.

2 Combine vinegar, water, sugar, salt, mustard seeds, coriander, and peppercorns in a small saucepan over medium heat. Bring to a simmer and stir until sugar and salt completely dissolve. Carefully pour contents over celery. Cool uncovered, then cover and refrigerate at least 24 hours.

MAKE THE BLUE CHEESE SAUCE:

Combine all ingredients in a medium bowl, stirring gently to combine. Cover and refrigerate until ready to serve.

MAKE THE BUFFALO SAUCE:

1 Place all ingredients except cornstarch mixture in a saucepan and stir to combine. Bring to a simmer over medium heat.

2 Whisk in cornstarch mixture. Remove pan from heat and cool. Keeps refrigerated up to 1 week.

FRY THE FROG LEGS AND SERVE:

1 Combine frog legs, milk, buttermilk, one-half teaspoon salt, and one-half teaspoon pepper in a medium bowl. Refrigerate at least 3 hours.

2 Meanwhile, blend remaining ingredients except oil in a medium bowl and set aside.

3 When ready to serve, heat oil in a deep-fat electric fryer to 350°F, or heat vegetable oil in a heavy 5-quart pot over medium-high heat until oil reaches 350°F.

4 Remove frog legs from buttermilk mixture and shake off excess. One at a time, lightly coat frog legs in cornmeal mixture, then dip back in buttermilk mixture, then in cornmeal mixture again. Gently place frog legs in hot oil and fry until golden brown. Drain on paper towels. Repeat until all legs are fried.

5 To serve, brush with Buffalo sauce and serve with a side of blue cheese dipping sauce and pickled celery.

BUFFALO SAUCE

2 teaspoons chile powder

1 teaspoon turmeric

1 teaspoon sweet paprika

1 teaspoon onion powder

1 teaspoon cayenne pepper

1 teaspoon coarse salt

2 teaspoons olive oil

2 teaspoons honey

2 teaspoons tomato paste

1 teaspoon smoked paprika

3 tablespoons apple cider vinegar

1 tablespoon garlic powder

1 tablespoon cornstarch blended with ½ cup cold water

FROG LEGS

8 frog legs

2 cups milk

2 cups buttermilk

1½ teaspoons salt, divided

2½ teaspoons coarsely ground black pepper, divided

1 tablespoon seafood seasoning, such as Old Bay

1 teaspoon onion powder

1 teaspoon garlic powder

1 cup all-purpose flour

1 cup cornmeal

1 quart vegetable oil

WHITING CAKES

SERVES 6 TO 8

1 to 1½ pounds whiting fillets

1 small to medium onion or large shallot, minced

¼ cup chopped fresh parsley

2 garlic cloves, minced

¼ cup mayonnaise

2 egg yolks, beaten

Coarse salt and pepper, to taste

Olive oil for sautéing

Ketchup, tartar sauce, or rémoulade (page 236), for serving

Lime wedges, for serving

WHEN YOU ASK JOURNALIST AND AVID FISHERMAN HANK CURTIS to share a recipe, you don't get a rudimentary culinary equation; you get a passionate narrative from a man who knows his fish and his way around a kitchen: "Whiting is one of Florida's most plentiful and easy-to-catch fish," Hank says. "A hand line or rod and reel, a couple of lead weights, a leader with three single hooks, a pocketful of sand fleas or some cut clam or shrimp, and dinner is almost ready." The best place to catch them is at the beach within a couple of feet of the surf line to thirty feet out in the Atlantic. No boat needed. "A rising tide in the morning or evening should produce enough whiting for lunch or dinner—and enough left over for sandwiches the next day."

Whiting is a mild-flavored, firm-fleshed fish that freezes well. It is simple to fillet, which makes preparation quick and easy. Hank likes to make cakes with whiting but says other fish will do. "Fish cakes are refrigerator- and pantry-friendly," he says. "Basically anything you find can be added to the mixture. If you catch blue fish, add chopped kalamata olives and feta for a nice balance with the stronger tasting fish. Capers work well, too. If you catch a couple of different types of fish, poach them and mix them together."

Hank serves these cakes with a sauce recipe from *Joy of Cooking* that blends 1½ cups sour cream, 2 tablespoons horseradish, the juice of half a lemon, 2 tablespoons chopped fresh dill, and coarse salt and pepper to taste.

1 Poach fish in hot, not boiling, water about 2 minutes, or until fillets are opaque. If skin was left on fillets, chill in refrigerator and strip flesh from skin. Break up fish by hand, checking for any bones; set aside.

2 Combine the fish, onion or shallot, parsley, and garlic in a bowl. Fold in mayonnaise, egg yolks, and salt and pepper to taste. Form into 6 to 8 cakes.

3 Heat oil in a large skillet over medium-high heat. Sauté cakes 5 to 6 minutes per side. Serve with lime wedges.

LEMON-HERB SWORDFISH SPIEDINI

| SERVES 4 |

---

1 tablespoon chopped fresh parsley

1 tablespoon finely chopped fresh rosemary

1 tablespoon extra-virgin olive oil, plus more for brushing

1 large lemon, zested and juiced

Coarse salt and freshly ground black pepper, to taste

1½ pounds swordfish steaks, cut into 2-inch cubes

Bamboo skewers, soaked in water for at least 1 hour

SWORDFISH IS ONE OF SEVERAL SPECIES OF BILLFISH that populate Florida's oceans. It's highly migratory and a prized catch for sport fishermen. It has a firm, meaty texture, which makes it perfect for the grill. Its mild flavor melds well with different flavors, including stronger herbs like rosemary that would overpower milder, flakier fish.

1 Combine parsley, rosemary, oil, lemon zest, and a pinch of salt and pepper in a large bowl, stirring to combine. Add swordfish cubes, tossing to coat. Cover tightly and refrigerate at least 3 hours and up to 6 hours.

2 Thread swordfish cubes onto skewers.

3 Preheat a large grill pan to medium-high. Brush pan with oil.

4 Place skewers on pan and sear 3 to 4 minutes, then flip and cook 3 to 4 minutes more, until swordfish is opaque and just cooked through. Sprinkle lemon juice over fish just before serving.

WHITE CLAM CHOWDER

SERVES 8 TO 10

THE HOMOSASSA RIVER HAS ALWAYS BEEN THE LIFEBLOOD of Old Homosassa. Herons gracefully glide from shore to shore. Cormorants pop their long necks out of the water, sometimes with a small fish speared in their beaks. Around one bend of the Otter Creek tributary, modern boaters find a snapshot of old Florida.

Set back in a small harbor is the Freezer Tiki Bar at Cedar Key Fish House. The old warehouse is where commercial fisherman brought their boats laden with crabs, fish, and shrimp. Guests arriving by car walk up a ramp to what once was the loading dock for trucks. To the left, the long, heavy plastic flaps that once protected the freezer entrance now cover the entryway to the Freezer Tiki Bar.

The Cedar Key Fish House is still a working wharf, but on weekends and at the height of scalloping season, the place is slammed with boaters, bikers, locals, and visitors seeking top-notch clam chowder, smoked mullet dip, spiced shrimp, and crabs—with ice cold beer to wash it all down. The service is as laid back as the surroundings, and menus are on large chalkboards throughout the room. Order at the counter to the side of the bar (cash only), grab a seat, and wait until they yell your name. The Freezer doesn't share its recipe for its tasty, super-thick clam chowder, but this is mighty close.

3 (8-ounce) bottles clam juice

1 pound Yukon gold potatoes, peeled and diced

3 tablespoons unsalted butter

2 cups chopped sweet onions

1¼ cups chopped fresh celery with leaves

½ cup chopped fresh parsley

2 garlic cloves, minced

1 bay leaf

¼ cup all-purpose flour

6 (6½-ounce) cans chopped clams, drained, juice reserved

2 cups heavy cream

3 ounces cream cheese, room temperature

¼ cup sour cream, optional

Milk, as needed

Coarse salt and pepper, to taste

Hot sauce, to taste

Oyster crackers for serving

1 Combine bottled clam juice and potatoes in a large saucepan over high heat and bring to a boil. Reduce heat to medium-low, cover pan, and simmer until potatoes are tender, about 10 minutes. Remove pan from heat.

2 Melt butter in a separate large saucepan over medium heat. Add onions, celery, parsley, garlic, and bay leaf and sauté until vegetables soften, about 6 minutes. Stir in flour and cook 2 minutes (do not allow flour to brown).

Gradually whisk in reserved juices from clams. Add potato mixture, clams, cream, cream cheese, and sour cream.

3 Simmer chowder 5 minutes to blend flavors, stirring frequently. Thin to desired consistency with milk, if needed. Season to taste with salt, pepper, and hot sauce. Serve with oyster crackers.

LOBSTER REUBEN

| MAKES 1 SANDWICH |

IT WAS THE LATE 1960S WHEN GARY GRAVES headed from chilly Wisconsin to the Florida Keys to scuba dive. The twenty-something loved the slow-paced life enough to stay and found a job at the newly opened Keys Fisheries in Marathon. Today he runs the multimillion-dollar operation, which is the largest processor of spiny lobster in the Florida Keys, with twenty-six fishermen bringing their daily catch during the annual lobster season from August through March.

Florida lobsters lack the large pinching claws of their Maine relatives and are beautifully marked with bright green, blue, and yellow spots on an orange or brown shell. Keys Fisheries boats harvest thousands of pounds daily at the height of the season, each lobster carefully measured while still in the water to be certain the carapace, or upper body, is at least three inches in length.

Gary is a walking encyclopedia about the life cycle of the Florida spiny lobster, a creature that makes it way on the Gulf Stream from far-off places—Cuba, Honduras, Nicaragua, Belize, and Brazil—to estuaries in the Keys. When spring comes, adult females spawn thousands of eggs in deep-sea waters. Those eggs grow to small larvae that are at the mercy of marine currents for almost a year before they become small lobsters. The sea movement takes them to the Keys' coast, where they grow, protected by coral, rocks, and vegetation.

Most lobsters are captured in the Florida Bay, not the ocean, says Gary. Fishermen set out empty traps and start pulling them after about five days, and no bait is needed: lobsters look for other lobsters, so if one is in a trap, others will climb right in. "They think it's a party," he explains. "In the wild, it's not unusual for sport divers to find twenty lobsters stacked in one hole."

Keys Fisheries operates a bayside restaurant that serves the bounty brought in year-round, including lobsters, stone crabs, golden crabs, and all sorts of fish. But the best seller by far is the lobster Reuben, which Graves says is inspired by a version created at Joe's Stone Crab in Miami (Joe's Stone Crab owns Keys Fisheries). The sweet, tender meat of the Florida lobster is all found in the tail.

> FLORIDA LOBSTERS LACK THE LARGE PINCHING CLAWS OF THEIR MAINE RELATIVES AND ARE BEAUTIFULLY MARKED WITH BRIGHT GREEN, BLUE, AND YELLOW SPOTS ON AN ORANGE OR BROWN SHELL.

1 Butter 1 side of each slice of bread. Place 1 slice, buttered side down, in a nonstick skillet over medium heat. Spread with 1 tablespoon dressing and top with lobster, Swiss cheese, and sauerkraut. Finish with remaining dressing and top with second slice of bread, buttered side up.

2 Grill until first side is golden, then flip and cook second side until cheese is melted and sandwich is heated through.

2 slices rye bread

2 tablespoons Thousand Island dressing, divided

¼ pound cooked Florida lobster

2 thin slices Swiss cheese

2 tablespoons prepared sauerkraut

Butter, for grilling

GUAVA-GLAZED MAHI MAHI
with COCONUT CURRY SAUCE

| SERVES 4 |

CHEECA LODGE AND SPA'S AUSPICIOUS HISTORY on Islamorada in the Florida Keys stretches over half a century, starting in 1946, when Clara Mae Downey from Olney, Maryland, opened the Olney Inn with twenty-two quaint bungalows. Her very first guest was President Harry Truman.

Fast forward to the 1960s, when the Olney Inn was rechristened Cheeca Lodge by its new owners, the Twitchell family. Cynthia Twitchell, better known as "Chee," was an heiress to the A&P grocery chain fortune and owner of a top thoroughbred racing farm. "We took my nickname, combined it with my husband Carl's, and came up with 'Cheeca,'" she recalls. The Twitchells added the main lodge, oceanfront villas, tennis courts, the golf course, and Cheeca's trademark wooden fishing pier. Chee raised miniature tarpon and seahorses in aquariums throughout the resort, and "Suzy the Seahorse" remains Cheeca's logo.

In the 1970s, when giant bonefish could still be reeled in right off the pier, outdoorsman and Coca-Cola magnate Carl Navarre purchased Cheeca Lodge. His celebrity pals, including Jack Paar, Paul Newman, Joanne Woodward, Jack Nicklaus, and President George H. W. Bush, flocked to the hotel for sportfishing.

Today, Cheeca Lodge is still a prime fishing spot, and if you're lucky enough to hook a fish, the kitchen will prepare your catch of the day for dinner.

This is one of the most popular dishes on the Cheeca Lodge menu. Mahi mahi is the Hawaiian name for the species *Coryphaena hippurus*, also known in Spanish as the dorado or in English as the dolphin fish—but it's very different from the bottlenose dolphin. The name, from Hawaiian origins, means "strong strong," referring to the mahi mahi's speed and agility. Its flavor is mild and sweet. Bamboo rice is a short-grain rice infused with green bamboo juice. It retains its bright jade-green color even after cooking. If you can't find it (look in specialty markets), you may substitute short-grain white rice. »

COCONUT CURRY SAUCE

2 green onions

2 shallots

1-inch piece fresh ginger

4 garlic cloves, smashed

1 stalk lemongrass, root end removed, smashed and chopped

2 tablespoons extra-virgin olive oil

1 Thai chile, chopped

1 tablespoon Thai red curry paste

1 teaspoon coriander seeds

2 sprigs fresh thyme

6 tablespoons light brown sugar, packed

1 cup dry vermouth

2 cups chicken stock

2 (14.5-ounce) cans coconut milk

½ cup chopped fresh cilantro

3 tablespoons fresh lemon juice

Coarse salt, to taste

GUAVA GLAZE

1½ cups guava paste or guava jelly

¼ cup soy sauce

1 tablespoon finely chopped fresh ginger

1 small jalapeño, seeds removed, finely chopped

MAKE THE COCONUT CURRY SAUCE:

1 Sauté green onions, shallots, ginger, garlic, and lemongrass in olive oil in a small saucepan for 2 minutes. Stir in Thai chile and curry paste and cook 5 minutes. Add coriander seeds, thyme, and brown sugar and cook for 2 minutes.

2 Deglaze pan with vermouth, then add chicken stock and simmer for 10 minutes, or until reduced by half. Add coconut milk and bring to a boil. Remove pan from heat and cool to room temperature.

3 Purée cooled sauce in blender and strain through a fine-mesh sieve. To serve, warm sauce and stir in fresh cilantro, lemon juice, and salt.

MAKE THE GUAVA GLAZE:

Warm all ingredients in a saucepan over low heat for 10 minutes, whisking until smooth. Pour glaze into blender and purée for 2 minutes. Strain through a fine-mesh sieve. Cover and refrigerate until ready to use.

COOK THE COCONUT BAMBOO RICE:

Combine all ingredients in a large saucepan, bring to a boil over high heat, reduce heat, cover, and simmer about 20 minutes, or until rice is cooked.

COOK THE BOK CHOY AND MAHI MAHI AND FINISH DISH:

1 Whisk flour, cornstarch, seltzer, and salt in a bowl large enough for dipping bok choy. Let stand 15 minutes.

2 Heat 2 tablespoons olive oil in a large sauté pan over medium-high heat until shimmering. Dip bok choy into batter, then fry until golden brown, about 2 minutes per side. Drain on paper towels and keep warm until ready to serve.

2 Preheat oven to 350°F. Heat remaining olive oil in a large sauté pan until it shimmers. Sear mahi mahi on both sides until golden. Place in oven to finish cooking, about 3 to 5 minutes (fish should flake but still be moist).

3 Remove pan from oven and cover fish with guava glaze. Return pan to oven for 1 minute.

4 To serve, place rice in center of each plate. Place fish on top of rice and ladle some of the coconut curry sauce around. Place bok choy on sauce.

COCONUT BAMBOO RICE

2 cups bamboo rice

1 teaspoon salt

1½ cups coconut milk

2 cups water

BOK CHOY AND MAHI MAHI

1 cup all-purpose flour

1 tablespoon cornstarch

1½ cups seltzer water

Pinch of salt

4 heads baby bok choy, halved, washed, and patted dry, stems intact

4 tablespoons olive oil, divided

4 (4- to 6-ounce) mahi mahi fillets

BROILED ROCK SHRIMP and CORN FRITTERS

| SERVES 6 |

FORTY YEARS AGO, ROCK SHRIMP WAS CONSIDERED a trash catch. They were called "peanuts" and "hard heads" because of their tough outer shell, and once opened, the crustaceans revealed a large sand vein that was anything but mouthwatering. But Titusville boat builder Rodney Thompson knew that once you got past all that, the rock shrimp flavor was something magical—the sweet, firm meat is often compared to miniature lobster tails, and some argue they're even tastier. Rodney's daughter Laurilee persuaded him to develop a way to easily shell and devein the tiny hard-shelled shrimp, and after some trial and error, Rodney invented a high-speed shell-splitting system, taking Florida rock shrimp from trash to treasure. The Thompsons eventually expanded their operations, opening Dixie Crossroads Seafood in Titusville.

The family, which includes more than six generations of fishermen, shrimpers, and shipbuilders, continues its culinary legacy with Wild Ocean Seafood Market in Titusville and Port Canaveral.

There are several ways to prepare rock shrimp, but our favorite way is the way Laurilee also likes them best: broiled and served with lemon wedges and plenty of clarified butter.

Fans of the Titusville seafood restaurant start each meal with these sugar-dusted fritters, but we like them right alongside—they bring out the sweetness in the broiled rock shrimp. To avoid overcooking the shrimp, the Thompsons suggest cooking just three shrimp at first to determine the exact cooking time for your oven. To clarify butter, melt it over low heat, spooning off the white solids as they rise to the top. And don't skimp on the shrimp—because they are small and oh so tasty, we can each easily eat a dozen (or two) for dinner! 》

MAKE THE FRITTERS:

1 Heat cooking oil to 350°F.

2 Sift together flour, baking powder, salt, and sugar in a large bowl. Combine eggs, milk, and butter in another bowl. Fold egg mixture into dry ingredients. Stir in corn.

3 Drop batter by tablespoons into hot oil and fry, turning periodically, until golden, about 5 minutes. Sprinkle with powdered sugar.

BROIL THE SHRIMP:

1 Position oven rack to highest position and preheat oven to broil.

2 To determine cooking time for shrimp, place 3 shrimp, shell side down, on a baking sheet. Brush lightly with clarified butter and sprinkle with seafood seasoning, if using.

3 Keep oven door slightly ajar to keep broiler on. Broil just until meat turns opaque and begins to curl away from the shell, 1½ to 3 minutes, depending on your oven.

4 Place remaining shrimp shell side down on the baking sheet and broil for the determined amount of time.

5 Serve with clarified butter and lemon wedges.

CORN FRITTERS

Vegetable oil for frying

2 cups all-purpose flour

1 tablespoon baking powder

½ teaspoon salt

4 tablespoons sugar

2 eggs, beaten

1 cup whole milk

4 tablespoons unsalted butter, melted and cooled

1 cup fresh corn kernels

Powdered sugar, for dusting

BROILED ROCK SHRIMP

6 dozen rock shrimp, split and cleaned

Clarified butter

Seafood seasoning, such as Old Bay, to taste (optional)

Lemon wedges, for serving

PEACE RIVER GATOR GUMBO

| SERVES 10 TO 15 |

PEACE RIVER SEAFOOD, AN ÜBERAUTHENTIC ROADSIDE CRAB SHACK just two miles off Interstate 75 in Punta Gorda, was a pioneer home in the 1920s, then a feed store. In 2003, Kelly Beall started serving alligator gumbo every Friday under a shady live oak as husband Jimmy's blue crab wholesale distribution facility sits behind the craftsman-style bungalow. While he worked, Kelly ladled up bowls of gumbo, drawing long lines of fans who showed up each week for the tender chunks of gator bathed in thick, spicy red stew.

Kelly retrofitted the old feed store with a kitchen, added blue crabs, then other locally caught seafood to her repertoire, and Peace River Seafood was born. During the season, hundreds of blue crabs from the Peace River are delivered daily to the back door, but Kelly's gator gumbo plays an Oscar-worthy supporting role. What's her secret?

"You gotta sing," says Kelly with a big smile. "Put some love in it." The real secret, however, is the roux, a mix of whole-wheat flour and butter that is stirred and tended over low heat "until it's the color of a penny." Add onions, green and red peppers, salt, pepper, garlic—"and sing," she reiterates, "just sing." "Serenade the marinade," says Peace River cook Larry Corbin, whom Kelly taught to make the gumbo. "Our kitchen is seasoned with love."

The gator simmers in a slow cooker with salt, pepper, and just enough chicken broth to keep it covered until fork tender. The broth is then stirred into the roux along with the gator meat, andouille sausage, crab, and shrimp. At the last minute, she adds fresh okra, "cooked just long enough to be tender," says Kelly.

While the blue crab wholesale is the heart of the business, the restaurant is the soul, with deep roots. "Buzz, one of our crabbers, goes back three generations," says Kelly. "And his granddad lived in this house in the 1940s."

Kelly grew up in nearby Fort Myers, the daughter of a commercial fisherman, and husband Jimmy grew up in Punta Gorda. They're keeping the Florida seafood legacy alive, with everything on the menu from Florida except the salmon, which Kelly trades for because her customers ask for it.

"We're serving the freshest seafood Florida offers," says Kelly. "And if you hear singing in the kitchen, you know we're hard at work."

Kelly's gumbo takes a couple of days to make properly. We added some fresh thyme, tomato paste, and celery leaves. The roux is best if it sits refrigerated overnight, and the gator needs to stew for hours so that the meat is tender. That's the real secret—along with singing.

~~~~~~

MAKE THE ROUX:

1 Melt butter in a large stockpot over low heat. Add flour and whisk constantly to a smooth consistency. Continue to cook until mixture is the color of a penny.

2 Stir in onions, peppers, and sausage and season to taste with salt, pepper, and cayenne. Let the roux cool to room temperature, then cover and refrigerate until ready to use.

MAKE THE GUMBO:

1 Place alligator in a pot or slow cooker and cover with water 2 inches above meat. Add bay leaf, celery leaves, thyme, pepper, salt, cayenne, and garlic. Cook, covered, on low for 4 hours, or until gator is tender enough to break apart with a fork.

2 Stir in shrimp and crab and cook through, about 10 minutes. Remove gator, shrimp, and crab, reserving liquid.

3 Stir chicken stock and seafood into cold roux, mixing well. Add reserved liquid from slow cooker, tomato paste, and okra. Cook just until okra is tender, about 15 minutes. Add additional chicken stock if needed to achieve desired consistency. Serve hot.

ROUX

1 cup unsalted butter

1 cup whole wheat flour

2 cups chopped sweet onions

2½ cups diced green bell pepper

1 pound andouille sausage, diced

Coarse salt, freshly ground black pepper, cayenne pepper, to taste

GATOR GUMBO

3 pounds gator, cut in 1-inch cubes

1 bay leaf

¼ cup chopped celery leaves

1 tablespoon fresh thyme

¼ cup coarsely ground black pepper

¼ cup salt

2 tablespoons cayenne pepper

2 tablespoons minced garlic

1 pound shrimp, peeled, deveined, and chopped small

½ pound crabmeat, lump or claw

½ cup chicken stock, plus more as needed

3 tablespoons tomato paste, or to taste

2 cups sliced okra

PARMESAN SNOOK

| SERVES 2 |

THIS PARADISE
FOR SPORTS
ANGLERS IS A
RICH FEEDING
GROUND FOR
BASS, TARPON,
SNOOK, REDFISH,
TROUT, PERMIT,
COBIA, SHARK,
GROUPER,
SNAPPER,
POMPANO,
SHEEPSHEAD,
TRIPLETAIL,
MACKEREL, AND
KINGFISH.

CHARLES WRIGHT MEETS US AS THE SUN RISES, and we board his fishing boat to head out of the tiny marina in Chokoloskee into the maze of mangroves and white-sand beaches known as the Ten Thousand Islands. Hugging the Everglades at the bottom of Florida's southwest coast, the watery wilderness spills into the Gulf of Mexico, tides moving in and out so quickly that the water ripples through myriad passes.

"This is like a 1.3-million acre classroom," says Charles, who guides anglers, paddlers, birders, and anyone interested in this matchless coastal ecosystem of salt marshes, estuaries, and mangrove forests. It's no territory for novices—the tangle of islands is a challenge to navigate, but he's been here on the water for seventeen years and intimately knows the landscape.

The largest mangrove forest in North America, Ten Thousand Islands is home to more than 400 species of fish, Charles says, and more than 200 species of birds. We spot roseate spoonbills, brown and white ibis, heron, snowy egrets, and a lone bald eagle—and only one other boat all morning.

The northern part of these beautifully desolate islands is in the Ten Thousand Islands National Wildlife Refuge, and the southern part is in Everglades National Park. The Calusa Indians were the first inhabitants, and their shell middens and pottery shards are still visible, Charles says. During the eighteenth century, the islands were a hideout for pirates, and stories of the area's notorious history as a smugglers' haven are legendary and easy to imagine as Charles winds through narrow passages and navigates shoals and hidden oyster bars. "Just makes sure you get back before dark," he says. Bobcats, marsh rabbits, snakes, and birds of prey survive on the bigger keys, so you want to carefully pick your campsite if you're overnighting.

The sheer abundance of life is remarkable—dolphins, turtles, manatees, and alligators make frequent appearances. We throw in a line and Charles hooks a silvery tarpon that gets away. This paradise for sports anglers is a rich feeding ground for bass, tarpon, snook, redfish, trout, permit, cobia, shark, grouper, snapper, pompano, sheepshead, tripletail, mackerel, and kingfish.

Charles says his two favorite meals are redfish and snook. He cooks redfish "on the half shell," simply filleted with skin and scales intact, then "shucked off the shell" after it's grilled or baked.

Snook, with its flaky, white meat and delicate flavor, is best eaten fresh. It's illegal to buy or sell, so if you want to eat one legally, you have to go out and catch it. (And you can only take one per day out of the water.) The Florida Fish and Wildlife Conservation Commission is very protective of Florida's premier game fish, found in big numbers only from Tampa south to the Keys. Charles's preferred method for snook is baked and topped with a rich sauce created by his wife, Vickie. Here is her recipe.

1 cup mayonnaise

3 to 5 chopped green onions, light green and white parts

½ to ¾ cup freshly grated Parmesan cheese

Dash of hot sauce

2 snook fillets, skin removed

3 tablespoons fresh lemon juice

1 Preheat oven to 350°F. Mix mayonnaise, green onions, cheese, and hot sauce in a small bowl and set aside.

2 Place snook in an ovenproof dish and pour lemon juice over it. Bake 10 minutes, or until almost done, depending on thickness of fillets. Remove dish from oven and spread topping evenly over filets. Turn oven to broil and place fish under broiler 2 to 3 minutes, until topping is bubbly and golden. Serve hot.

EVERGLADES NATIONAL PARK

EVERGLADES NATIONAL PARK spans 1.5 million acres of tropical and subtropical habitat and has one of the world's most diverse ecosystems. The mosaic of shallow ponds, clumps of palms, slow-moving streams, sawgrass marshes, hardwood hammocks, and mangrove forests was created over thousands of years.

Shaped by human-made and lightning-sparked fires, the ebb and flow of water, and wind whipped from hurricanes, the Everglades have been declared an International Biosphere Reserve, a World Heritage Site, and a Wetland of International Importance, one of only three locations in the world to appear on all three lists.

More than 275 species of fish are known from the Everglades, most inhabiting the marine and estuarine waters. Snook, largemouth bass, redfish, catfish, bluegill, red snapper, and tarpon attract thousands of anglers every year.

The northernmost headwaters of the Everglades stretch to Shingle Creek near Orlando. From there a patchwork of waterways make a slow 200-mile trek south. At one time the Everglades covered much of southern Florida. Native Americans, who planted on these islands, called them *hammocka*, the "garden place." When the Europeans came, they thought of the vast region as "glades." Today the Everglades and Francis S. Taylor Wildlife Management Area are part of what remains of the largest freshwater marsh ecosystem in the United States.

HEIRLOOM TOMATO and CORNBREAD PANZANELLA

| SERVES 8 |

1 cup finely ground cornmeal

1 cup all-purpose flour

1 tablespoon baking powder

1 teaspoon coarse salt

½ teaspoon coarsely cracked black pepper

1 tablespoon sugar

¼ cup finely chopped, seeded jalapeño pepper

¾ cup grated extra-sharp cheddar cheese

1 egg

1 cup buttermilk

4 tablespoons unsalted butter, melted

4 large heirloom tomatoes

2 large cucumbers, peeled, halved lengthwise, and seeded

2 ears fresh corn, shucked

½ medium red onion, peeled

2 tablespoons fresh lemon juice

1 teaspoon red wine vinegar

¼ cup extra-virgin olive oil

Coarse salt and freshly ground black pepper, to taste

OUR FAVORITE COMPONENT OF THIS SALAD is the cornbread soaked in the delicious lemony dressing and the juices from the tomatoes. You can make this up to thirty minutes ahead of time, but don't let it go much past that or the cornbread will start to fall apart. To save a little bit of time, you can make the cornbread the night before.

1 Preheat oven to 400°F. Grease an 8-inch square baking pan and set aside.

2 Whisk together cornmeal, flour, baking powder, salt, pepper, and sugar in a large bowl. Stir in jalapeños and cheese. Make a well in center of mixture.

3 Whisk together egg, buttermilk, and melted butter in a medium bowl. Pour egg mixture into well in cornmeal mixture and stir gently until batter is blended and no lumps remain.

4 Spoon batter into prepared pan. Bake until a tester inserted in center comes out clean, 20 to 25 minutes.

5 Transfer pan to a wire rack and cool to room temperature.

6 Cut cornbread in half widthwise, then cut each half into 6 strips. Cut strips into 1½-inch cubes.

7 Preheat oven to 250°F. Place cornbread cubes on a baking sheet and bake until dry and crisp, about 35 minutes. Set aside to cool completely.

8 Cut tomatoes into wedges. Slice cucumber. Cut corn kernels from cobs, discarding cobs. Shave red onion into thin half-moon shapes using a mandoline or V-slicer or a vegetable peeler.

9 Whisk together lemon juice, vinegar, and oil in the bottom of a large serving bowl. Season to taste with salt and pepper. Set aside 10 to 30 minutes before serving.

10 Add tomatoes, cucumbers, and onion to dressing, tossing to coat. Add cornbread cubes, tossing gently to combine. Season to taste with salt and pepper.

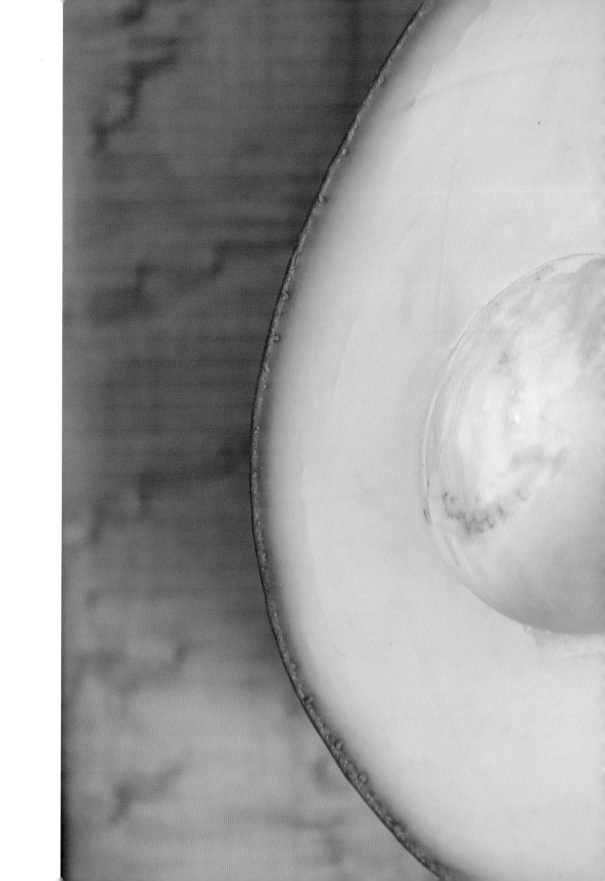

EDAMAME, AVOCADO, and PEPITAS SALAD

| SERVES 6 TO 8 |

FLORIDA AVOCADOS HAVE MORE WATER than their California counterparts, but they're just as delicious. You can make this up to one day ahead of time, but if you do, leave out the avocado and stir it in just before serving.

1 In a bowl large enough for the salad, whisk together the vinegar, salt, pepper, mustard, lemon juice, and olive oil. Add the diced red onions and set aside.

2 Prepare edamame according to package directions; rinse with cold water and cool to room temperature. Add edamame, carrots, radishes, celery, avocado, and pepitas to the vinaigrette, tossing to combine. Season to taste with salt and pepper and garnish with fresh tarragon leaves.

¼ cup champagne vinegar

Coarse salt and freshly ground black pepper, to taste

1 teaspoon Dijon mustard

1 tablespoon fresh lemon juice

¼ cup olive oil

¼ cup finely diced red onion

1 (16-ounce) bag frozen shelled edamame

½ cup finely diced carrot

½ cup finely diced red radish

½ cup finely diced celery

1 ripe Florida avocado, diced

½ cup roasted, hulled pepitas (pumpkin seeds)

Fresh tarragon, for garnish

GRILLED LEMON OKRA

THIS IS THE PERFECT PLACE TO USE A GRILL BASKET if you have one. The okra can also be skewered to keep them from falling through the grill. Using soaked six-inch wooden skewers, spear three to four okra together, securing at the top and bottom of the pods with skewers. This will make the okra easy to turn on the grill.

1 pound okra, washed, dried, stems trimmed

1 tablespoon extra-virgin olive oil

Coarse salt to taste

1 teaspoon finely grated fresh lemon zest

1 tablespoon fresh lemon juice

1 Heat a gas or charcoal grill to high.

2 Toss okra with oil and place on grill. Cover and cook until grill marks or charred edges appear, about 5 minutes. Turn okra, cover, and cook until tender, about 5 minutes more.

3 Place okra in serving dish. Sprinkle with salt, lemon zest, and lemon juice. Toss with tongs before serving.

JICAMA and RED CABBAGE SLAW

JICAMA (HEE-KA-MA) HAS THE CRUNCH OF A WATER CHESTNUT and the slightly sweet flavor of a green apple. Also called a Mexican potato, jicama can be used as you would water chestnuts in seafood stir-fries or to add fresh flavor to salads. It's an unexpected addition to this coleslaw, which has just enough bite from the radishes and green onions and a lighter-than-usual dressing made with sour cream instead of mayo.

3 cups peeled, shredded jicama

3 cups grated red cabbage

½ cup grated radishes

¼ cup thinly sliced green onion, white and light green parts

¼ cup plus 2 tablespoons fresh lime juice

¾ cup vegetable oil

½ cup sour cream

Coarse salt and freshly ground black pepper, to taste

Cayenne pepper, to taste

1 Place jicama, cabbage, radishes, and onions in large serving bowl.

2 Mix lime juice, oil, sour cream, salt, pepper, and cayenne in small bowl. Pour over jicama-cabbage mixture. Toss to blend.

3 Chill at least 4 hours before serving.

ORANGE—SOUR CREAM COFFEE CAKE

MAKES 1 (9 X 13-INCH) CAKE

CAKE

¾ cup orange juice, divided

1½ cups unsalted butter, softened, divided

3 cups all-purpose flour, divided

1½ cups light brown sugar, packed

2 tablespoons ground cinnamon

1½ cups roughly chopped pecans

1 cup sugar

2 eggs

1 cup sour cream

1 tablespoon orange zest

1 teaspoon baking powder

1 teaspoon baking soda

½ teaspoon salt

ORANGE GLAZE

2 cups confectioner's sugar

¾ cup orange juice

THIS TENDER, MOIST COFFEE CAKE was pirated from Pam's grandmother's recipe box. It can serve as dessert, but you can also prep it the night before, then bake and pack along for breakfast on a fishing trip when you need something sturdy that travels well. The sweet aroma will get your day going—have a piece while it's warm with a strong cup o' joe.

MAKE THE CAKE:

1 Preheat oven to 350°F. Butter and flour a 13 x 9 x 2-inch baking pan.

2 Combine one-quarter cup orange juice, three-quarters cup butter, three-quarters cup flour, brown sugar, cinnamon, and pecans, mixing until crumbly. Set aside.

2 Beat remaining three-quarters cup butter and sugar in a large bowl until light and fluffy. Add eggs, sour cream, remaining one-half cup orange juice, and orange zest, mixing well.

3 Combine remaining 2¼ cups flour, baking powder, baking soda, and salt in a separate bowl. Add to butter mixture and blend well. Pour into prepared pan.

4 Spread evenly with crumb topping.

5 Bake 35 to 40 minutes, or until a cake tester inserted near the center comes out clean. Remove from oven and cool slightly. Turn out onto wire rack.

6 Place wire rack in a baking sheet lined with parchment paper. Drizzle glaze over cake.

MAKE THE ORANGE GLAZE:

Combine orange juice and confectioner's sugar in a small bowl, whisking until smooth.

PEANUT BUTTER–CHOCOLATE PIE

| MAKES ONE 9-INCH PIE |

NO MATTER WHAT YOU EAT, THOUGH, WE RECOMMEND ENDING THE MEAL WITH A SLICE OF THEIR LEGENDARY PEANUT BUTTER– CHOCOLATE PIE.

MICK JAGGER STAYED HERE. SO DID ERNEST HEMINGWAY. Imagine John Wayne sipping cocktails on the wide screened porch of the weathered Rod and Gun Club, a jewel in Everglades City, Florida's last, lonely frontier on the western edge of Everglades National Park.

Anglers and birders discovered the retreat in the 1880s, when only small boats and yachts could navigate Chokoloskee Bay and the Barron River, which today still teem with grouper, pompano, redfish, shrimp, Florida lobster, stone crab, and mullet. The club was built onto the original trading post, erected by the first permanent white settler, who founded the town in 1864.

Among regular guests at the turn of the twentieth century was tycoon Barron G. Collier, who bought the retreat in 1922 as a hunting and fishing club for wealthy northerners. Through the decades, Presidents Roosevelt, Truman, Hoover, Eisenhower, Nixon, and Bush Sr. visited here, escaping to a simple life of fishing and relaxing on the lodge's wide screened porch overlooking the Barron River.

Collier died in 1939, and his heirs sold the club in 1960. Today, the Bowen family runs the three-story white clapboard lodge, the only original structure to survive a 1969 fire. Stepping through the worn back door is like walking into another era—lobby walls paneled in dark pecky cypress decorated with trophy catches of game fish and wildlife, and a smoothly worn marble registration desk. Antique mariners' maps, rifles, and framed newspaper clippings dating back 100 years are reminders of the club's epic history.

Today, the upper floors of the lodge are closed, with accommodations in five tidy cabins adjacent to the main building, perfect for guests who are there for one reason: to hook a tarpon, snook, or redfish in the nearby Everglades and Ten Thousand Islands.

Seasonal fish is always on the menu, but the best meal of all is when the cooks grill, blacken, or fry your own catch. No matter what you eat, though, we recommend ending the meal with a slice of their legendary peanut butter–chocolate pie. Owner Patty Bowen shared the recipe. »

8 ounces chocolate wafer cookies, finely crushed to make 2 cups

2 to 4 tablespoons unsalted butter

½ cup heavy whipping cream

1 teaspoon vanilla extract

½ cup light brown sugar, packed

¾ cup creamy peanut butter

8 ounces cream cheese, room temperature

½ cup semisweet chocolate chunks

½ cup chopped peanuts, for garnish

1 Preheat oven to 350°F.

2 For the crust, stir together cookie crumbs and butter in a small bowl with a fork. Press into a 9-inch pie pan and bake 5 to 7 minutes. Remove from oven and cool on a rack.

3 For filling, beat whipping cream, gradually adding vanilla and sugar, until stiff peaks form. Set aside.

4 Combine peanut butter and cream cheese until smooth in a large bowl. Stir in chocolate chunks. Add half of whipped cream to peanut butter mixture, folding by hand until blended.

5 Pour peanut butter mixture over cookie crumb crust. Top with remaining whipped cream and garnish with chopped peanuts. Chill at least 1 hour before serving.

Winter's
ABUNDANCE

COLA OYSTERS · SEA TROUT · STONE CRAB · ROGFISH · KALE · ORANGES · GRAPEFRUITS · LEMONS

TOES • APALACHICOLA OYSTERS • SEA TROUT • STONE CRAB • HOGFISH • KALE • ORANGES • GRAPEFRU

MOSCOW MULE

| MAKES 1 DRINK |

½ **juicy lime**

¼ **cup vodka**

½ **to ¾ cup spicy ginger beer**

TRADITIONALLY SERVED IN A COPPER MUG, the Moscow mule is a favorite of our book's talented photographer, Diana Zalucky. Ginger beer is far less sweet than ginger ale and has a more up-front ginger flavor. Look for it in liquor stores and in large supermarkets—it's definitely worth seeking out for this drink.

Squeeze lime into the bottom of a copper mug or highball glass. Add 3 large ice cubes. Pour in vodka and cold ginger beer, stirring to combine.

SUNDOWNER PUNCH

| MAKES 1 DRINK |

2 cups aged rum, chilled

3 cups dry orange soda, chilled

2 cups fresh blood orange juice, chilled

3 dashes bitters

THIS COCKTAIL GOT ITS NAME FOR TWO REASONS: first, blood orange juice gives it the fiery coral hue of a sunset on the beach; second, it's an ideal quaff for sipping with friends as the sun goes down. Look for dry orange soda in liquor stores, or substitute a high-quality orange soda such as Orangina or San Pellegrino Aranciata.

Stir together rum, soda, juice, and bitters in a large pitcher. Serve punch over ice, preferably at sunset.

GRILLED OCTOPUS with POTATOES

| SERVES 4 |

THOUGH IT ISN'T USUALLY COMMERCIALLY AVAILABLE, octopus is caught in Florida waters by spearfishermen. It may seem intimidating, but octopus is easy to cook, and when you bite into the tender meat that tastes so much like the sea, you'll agree it's worth overcoming any reluctance to cook fresh octopus. The trick is in the long simmer, which tenderizes the otherwise chewy tentacles. It's ready to eat at that point, but tossing it on the grill adds an extra layer of flavor.

2 to 3 pounds Florida octopus, cleaned

1 cup dry white wine

4 medium Yukon gold potatoes, cut into ½-inch slices

¼ cup extra-virgin olive oil

2 teaspoons smoked paprika, plus additional for garnish

½ teaspoon coarse salt

Freshly ground black pepper, to taste

2 tablespoons chopped fresh parsley

1　Place octopus in a large pot with a lid. Add wine, then cover with enough water to reach 1 inch above octopus.

2　Cover and bring to a boil over high heat. Lower heat to medium and simmer 45 minutes to 1 hour, or until a knife inserted in the thickest part of the octopus meets no resistance.

3　Remove octopus from cooking liquid and place in a large bowl. Keep cooking liquid at a simmer.

4　Place potatoes in simmering water for 3 minutes, or until just tender but still holding together. Remove from water and place on a baking sheet lined with paper towels to drain.

5　Preheat grill to medium-high.

6　Combine oil, paprika, salt, and pepper in a medium bowl. Pour about half of oil mixture over octopus, tossing to coat. Brush remaining oil on potatoes.

7　Carefully place octopus on grill. Grill, turning often, until charred in places, about 4 minutes total. Remove from grill and set aside.

8　Place potatoes on grill. Grill until tender, about 2 minutes per side. Remove from grill and set aside.

9　Cut octopus into 1-inch-thick slices. Arrange potatoes on a serving dish. Top with octopus and garnish with parsley and a sprinkle of smoked paprika.

OYSTER STEW

| SERVES 6 TO 8 |

1 pint shucked oysters in their liquor

½ stick unsalted butter

1 bunch green onions, white and light green parts only, chopped

3 cups whole milk

3 cups heavy cream

Coarse salt and freshly ground black pepper, to taste

Paprika, for garnish

A SIGN INSIDE THE DOOR OF BOSS OYSTER in Apalachicola reads, "Welcome to oystertown . . . your oyster is our world." The Boss, as locals call it, is synonymous with Florida oysters. Served raw, roasted, or baked and topped with a myriad of flavors from bacon and jalapeños to mushrooms and feta, the bivalves are harvested in Apalachicola Bay from the restaurant's own boat every day. The restaurant's no-frills open-air rooms and waterfront setting are exactly what you'd expect to find in this little old oystering town.

There are 7,000 acres of oyster beds in the 210 square miles of Apalachicola Bay. With a deeply cupped shell, balanced saltiness, and plump, meaty texture, the oysters from Apalachicola are prized by chefs and oyster aficionados around the country. Ninety percent of Florida's oysters come from here; however, due to excessive drought conditions in the bay caused by a dwindling supply of water from two rivers that start in Georgia, oyster harvest has seen a marked decline over the last few years.

Freshly shucked oysters should have a pleasant sea breeze aroma. Shells should not be cracked and should close when they are tapped. When fully cooked, oysters become plump and opaque, and their edges begin to curl.

It seems as though everyone in Apalachicola has a recipe for oyster stew. Here's our simple take on the classic creamy soup.

1 Strain oysters from liquor; place oysters in a small bowl and refrigerate. Pour oyster liquor through a fine sieve lined with a paper towel into a separate small bowl; set aside.

2 Melt butter in a large saucepan over medium heat. Add green onions, cooking until tender, about 3 minutes.

3 Add milk, cream, and reserved oyster liquor. Bring to a simmer over medium heat, then add oysters. Reduce heat to low and cook until edges of oysters begin to curl, about 1 minute.

4 Season to taste with salt and pepper and garnish each bowl with a sprinkle of paprika.

SPICY CONCH CHOWDER

| SERVES 6 |

KEY LARGO CONCH HOUSE IS A FAMILY AFFAIR, a serendipitous labor of love for the Dreaver family, who migrated south in 2003 and opened the little eatery on Key Largo so they all could live close to the ocean. Ted and Laura Dreaver, sons Jonathan and Justin, and daughter Stephanie all play a role in the day to day. Even though the queen conch is found in the waters around the Florida Keys, the species is protected. Still, visitors and locals clamor for a taste of the sweet, chewy meat, so the Dreavers keep it on the menu and source from the Caribbean (you can buy frozen conch meat in many Florida fish markets).

While their conch fritters have been featured on network television, it was the spicy conch chowder Pam most appreciated on her visit. You can turn up the heat with cayenne and serve with your favorite hot sauce.

1 pound conch, cleaned and finely chopped

5 small potatoes, such as Yukon gold, peeled and diced

1 small red onion, finely chopped

½ cup finely chopped celery

½ cup finely chopped carrots

4 garlic cloves, minced

1 bay leaf

¼ cup chopped fresh cilantro

4 cups chicken stock

2 (28-ounce) cans diced tomatoes and juice

1 cup tomato juice

Coarse salt and freshly ground black pepper, to taste

Cayenne pepper, to taste

Combine all ingredients in a large pot over high heat, stirring well to combine. Bring to a boil, reduce heat, and simmer 1 hour. Discard bay leaf. Season with salt, pepper, and cayenne to taste.

OYSTER SHOOTERS

| SERVES 4 |

4 teaspoons finely chopped peeled and seeded cucumber, divided

4 raw oysters

½ cup tequila, chilled

2 teaspoons fresh lime juice

Pinch coarse salt

Ice

2 teaspoons finely minced fresh cilantro, divided

Hot sauce, to taste

WHILE WE THINK OF APALACHICOLA as the epicenter of Florida oystering, Sarasota Bay on the Gulf Coast once supported a thriving oyster community. Though more than a century of growth and development killed off many of the area's oyster beds, oyster houses still abound on the bay, keeping the mollusk part of the area's history. And serious work is under way by the Sarasota Bay Estuary Program to restore the beds.

Along the Gulf Coast, oysters are still harvested in the same way they have been for more than a century—from small boats by fishermen using large, long-handled tongs to scoop them up from their beds in the shallow water. Hand tonging is backbreaking work, but it's much more sustainable than dredging, which heavily damages oyster beds.

Among Florida's top commercial seafood products in terms of dockside value, oysters are valuable in many other ways, too: they play a critical role in their ecosystems, filtering and cleaning the water, helping stabilize the coastline, and providing habitat for fish, shrimp, crabs, and other animals.

When you get a fresh, briny oyster that's just been shucked, there's no better way to enjoy it than raw. An oyster shooter is a bracing way to start a meal. These are fun for parties, too—the recipe easily doubles or triples to serve more.

1 Place 1 teaspoon chopped cucumber in the bottom of 4 tall shot glasses. Top each with 1 oyster.

2 Combine tequila, lime juice, and salt in a cocktail shaker with ice; shake a few times until mixture is cold. Strain mixture into glasses over oysters.

3 Top with cilantro and hot sauce to taste.

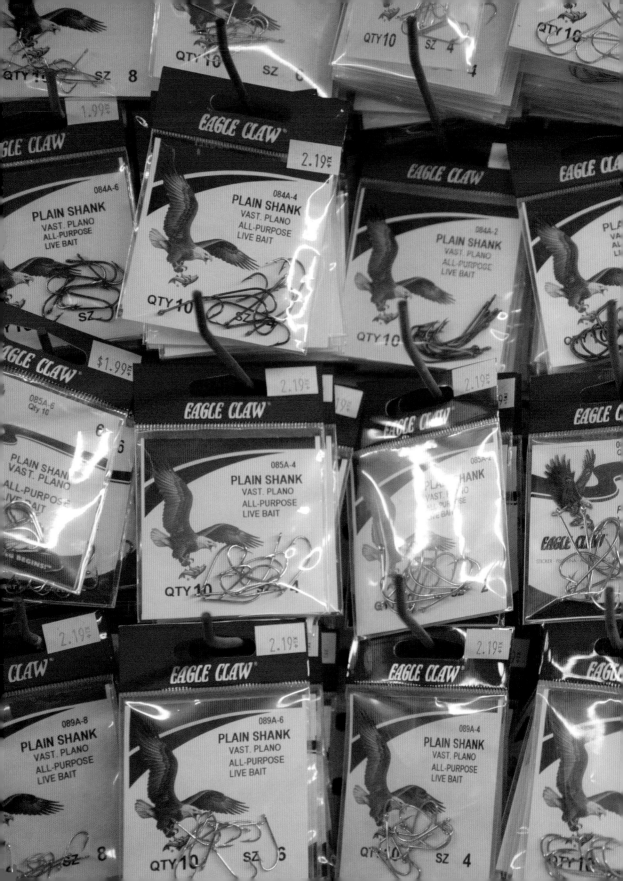

CINTHIA SANDOVAL

SPANISH-STYLE BROILED MACKEREL

| SERVES 4 |

AT WILD OCEAN SEAFOOD MARKET'S Port Canaveral docks and market, the early-morning air has the subtle fresh aroma of the ocean. A well-worn shrimp trawler rests easy at the dock. The seas are calm, and the boat's haul of rock shrimp is already packed in bags and on ice.

Clad in rubber boots and skinny jeans, Cinthia Sandoval wheels over an ice-filled tub stacked with a variety of fish caught just the day before. She grabs a huge red snapper by its gills, scales glimmering in the sun, and explains that while clear eyes can tell you the fish is fresh, clean-smelling gills are really the best way to know. Though her official title is marketing manager, there isn't much Cinthia doesn't do at Wild Ocean. Her passion for the job is evident. Inside the small dockside market, she confidently rattles off the names of all of the seafood on ice—a gorgeous array of Spanish mackerel, spindly golden crab, black bass, luminescent butterfish, tripletail, silvery pompano, and more.

For more than four generations, the Thompson family and Wild Ocean have provided locally caught seafood from the Atlantic Coast. Most of the inventory goes straight from their boats to market, including a larger market in nearby Titusville that houses both their retail fish shop and their fish-processing facility. Workers sit at long stainless steel tables methodically hand peeling shrimp, scaling and filleting fish, and processing the tiny rock shrimp that put the Thompson family on the map with a brilliantly simple machine designed by family patriarch, Rodney Thompson, that splits the hard shell and removes the thick vein of sand.

Wild Ocean has been a longtime leader in sustainability, and Cinthia is a leader in local initiatives. "People don't realize how fragile our ecosystem is," she says. "Everything is intertwined. If we aren't aware of our environment, if we aren't diligent about green practices, our food supply will be in peril. At Wild Ocean sustainability is our business."

Cinthia doesn't write down recipes, so she recited her favorite quick way to prepare fish—a simple, Spanish-inspired broiled mackerel that she says she makes at least once a week. 》

"PEOPLE DON'T REALIZE HOW FRAGILE OUR ECOSYSTEM IS. EVERYTHING IS INTERTWINED. IF WE AREN'T AWARE OF OUR ENVIRONMENT, IF WE AREN'T DILIGENT ABOUT GREEN PRACTICES, OUR FOOD SUPPLY WILL BE IN PERIL."

4 (6-ounce) Spanish mackerel fillets, skin on

1 tablespoon plus 2 teaspoons extra-virgin olive oil, divided

1 teaspoon ground cumin

¼ teaspoon coarse salt, plus additional to taste

1 large Spanish onion, thinly sliced

1 large tomato, diced

¼ cup capers

2 tablespoons fresh lime juice

Freshly ground black pepper, to taste

1 Place oven rack 5 to 6 inches from heat and preheat broiler.

2 Line a baking sheet with parchment paper. Place mackerel fillets skin side down on prepared baking sheet. Brush lightly with 2 teaspoons oil, then evenly sprinkle with cumin and salt.

3 Broil fish with oven door slightly ajar 3 to 4 minutes, or until it just turns opaque. Loosely tent fish with foil and set aside.

4 Heat remaining 1 tablespoon oil in a large skillet. Add onions, cooking until softened, about 4 minutes. Stir in tomato, cooking until juicy and softened, 2 to 3 minutes. Stir in capers and lime juice and season with salt and pepper to taste.

5 Spoon sauce over mackerel and serve immediately.

"THE BEST FISHERMAN ALONG THE FLORIDA COAST"

KNOWN AS ONE OF THE FINEST GUIDES ever to take visitors out to sea for a guaranteed catch, Jesse Linzy was a fishing legend in the early 1900s in the little town of Ponce Park. He fished in a heavy wooden boat, single-handedly rowing guests through the treacherous inlet, often against the tide. Jesse knew all the best places to drop a line and made sure his anglers had a catch.

Standing six feet eight inches tall, usually bare-chested and wearing faded dungarees, Jesse was extraordinarily strong and lithe and rarely seen without a fishing pole. His hands were enormous and his feet so large that even the biggest shoes had the ends cut off so that his toes would fit, according to documents at the Ponce de Leon Inlet Lighthouse Preservation Association.

Jesse likely came to Florida from Georgia as a young man around 1909 to work on construction projects at the Ponce Inlet Lighthouse. He built the sidewalk from the tower down to the river, and it is still there today.

Besides his work as a fishing guide and handyman at the Pacetti Hotel near the Mosquito (now Ponce) Inlet Lighthouse, Jesse also worked as an assistant to Bartola John "Bert" Pacetti, who had become a federal bird reservation inspector. Jesse traveled around the country with Bert to places as far-flung as Alaska and Hawaii.

By 1935, the Pacetti Hotel had fallen into disrepair and was purchased by Olivia Gamble, who had vacationed there as a child. Jesse and his wife, Miss Ida, lived in the hotel and took care of Olivia and her guests. (His bed is now in the collection of the Ponce Inlet Lighthouse and can be seen on display in the first assistant keeper's dwelling.)

An African American in Florida just seven years after the Civil War, when the country was still divided on race, Jesse worked in a profession that depended on well-heeled tourists to hire him and follow his instructions for fishing. And listen they did. It's said he took no nonsense from tourists, and a tardy angler was likely to find Jesse relaxing in a hammock, the fishing trip canceled.

Except for his travels with Bert Pacetti, Jesse spent his life in the small Florida town until he died in 1955 at age eighty-three. "He was affectionately known not only as the mayor but also as the giant of Ponce Park," reads his obituary. "He was also known from north to south as the best fisherman along the Florida coast."

JESSE LINZY

SAUTÉED SHAD ROE ON CROSTINI

| SERVES 2 |

¼ cup unsalted butter

2 lobes fresh shad roe

¼ cup dry white wine

¼ cup fresh lemon juice

¼ cup chopped fresh dill

Coarse sea salt and freshly ground black pepper, to taste

4 medium slices ciabatta bread, lightly toasted

SHAD, A FISH MANY CONSIDER TO BE BAIT AND NOTHING MORE, spawn in the St. Johns River from late December through late February or early March. Most of the spawning takes place in "Shad Alley," a stretch of river from Lake Monroe to Lemon Bluff. Shad's high fat content makes the flesh tender and very tasty. According to the Florida Fish and Wildlife Conservation Commission, the fish's Latin name, *A. sapidissima*, translates as "most savory."

The flesh may be delectable, but it's full of hundreds of tiny bones, which makes eating it a chore. In fact, a Native American legend says that a porcupine fled into the water and was turned inside out to become the shad. It's that bony. If you can find a fishmonger who fillets and bones shad, consider yourself lucky—it's rare to find someone with the skill and patience to remove the thousands of pinbones in the fish.

So rather than go through all the trouble of removing all those pesky bones, we prefer to eat the roe, which is prized for its meaty texture and singularly rich flavor. Roe is harvested when the shad spawn, which happens in Florida in late winter rather than spring, since our waters warm earlier. Look for fresh shad roe in small fish markets. If you don't see it, ask your fishmonger to source it for you. Chances are, they know where to find it.

1 Melt butter in a small sauté pan with a lid over medium-low heat. Add roe, cover, and sauté 5 minutes. Carefully flip roe and sauté 5 minutes more. Remove roe from pan and set aside.

2 Turn heat to medium-high. Add white wine and lemon juice and cook, stirring, 3 to 4 minutes. Stir in dill and salt and pepper, to taste. Return roe to pan, turning to coat in sauce. Remove from heat.

3 Slice roe into 1-inch pieces and serve on toasted ciabatta, spooning sauce over top.

SEA TROUT ROMESCO

| SERVES 4 |

SEA TROUT IS NOT ACTUALLY A TROUT, but a member of the drum family. It's likely someone saw the resemblance to the freshwater fish and gave it the nickname. Its flavor and texture are also quite similar to that of freshwater trout: the thin fillets are sweet and tender and flake easily. The romesco sauce is actually best when made a day ahead of serving. Cover tightly and refrigerate, then bring to room temperature before serving.

¾ cup sliced almonds

½ cup French bread cubes, toasted

½ cup plus 2 tablespoons olive oil, divided

1 (15-ounce) can diced fire-roasted tomatoes with juice

1 (8-ounce) jar roasted red peppers, drained

3 tablespoons red wine vinegar

1 tablespoon paprika

1 teaspoon coarse salt, plus additional for seasoning fish

½ teaspoon freshly ground black pepper, plus additional for seasoning fish

4 (6-ounce) fillets fresh sea trout

Fresh chives, for garnish

1 Preheat oven to 350°F.

2 Toss almonds and bread cubes with one-quarter cup oil in a large bowl; spread on a baking sheet and toast 5 minutes, or until golden brown.

3 Combine toasted bread and almonds, one-quarter cup oil, tomatoes and juice, roasted peppers, vinegar, paprika, salt, and pepper in a food processor and process until smooth. Cover romesco tightly and refrigerate at least 30 minutes and up to overnight.

4 Heat remaining 1 tablespoon oil in a large sauté pan over medium-high heat. Season trout with salt and pepper. Working in batches and using remaining oil as needed, gently place trout in oil, skin side down. Cook 3 to 4 minutes; turn fish and cook 2 to 3 minutes longer, or until fish is just opaque and springs back when touched lightly.

5 Spoon romesco in center of plate, top with a trout fillet, and garnish with chives.

LOBSTER CREOLE

| SERVES 2 |

IN A CITY WHERE DINING TRENDS ARE BORN, Garcia's Seafood Grille & Fish Market is an old-school classic along the river in downtown Miami, where celebrities rub elbows with everyday folks who frequent Garcia's for simple, fresh seafood.

It's a familiar tale of Cuban exile—eleven Garcia brothers born into a family of fishermen in the province of Las Villas, Cuba, left their home in 1964 to escape the Castro regime and start a new life in America doing what they knew best: fishing. By 1966, they had saved enough money to open a fish market, processing plant, and wholesale business along the Miami River with their own small fleet of fishing boats and launched Garcia Brothers Seafood. In 1976, they added a counter and a deep fryer and started serving their daily catch.

Today Garcia's harvests more than 10,000 stone crab traps and 15,000 lobster traps, and the casual restaurant is now two stories with a cocktail bar and dining rooms in addition to the waterside tables that made it famous. The family has amicably split the restaurant business, and Garcia's is operated by Esteban Garcia's two sons, Luis and Esteban. Their mother, María Luisa, holds court at the fish counter and makes each perfect cup of thick, rich Cuban coffee that leaves the kitchen.

It's a place that sticks to the basics—whole fried yellowtail frequently comes out of the kitchen, or piles of fresh stone crabs, or broiled, stuffed lobster. A chalkboard menu on the outside porch lists the catches of the day, and the tiny kitchen serves seafood mostly grilled or fried. Simple sides—yellow rice, sweet or green plantains, coleslaw—are all homemade and all prepared under the watchful eye of María Luisa.

"We want you to leave here feeling like you came to our home," Luis says. "As my dad used to say, when it's fresh, keep it simple."

Lobster creole is a house specialty and comes together in minutes—a delicious way to stretch a lobster tail to feed two. Garcia's serves it with a side of yellow rice and sweet plantains. Pam watched the cook put it together in minutes on the stovetop. Here is our version. 》

1 spiny Florida lobster tail, shell on

2 tablespoons extra-virgin olive oil, divided

2 tablespoons chopped red bell pepper

2 tablespoons chopped green bell pepper

2 tablespoons chopped red onion

1 cup chopped fresh tomato with juice

2 tablespoons Sazón seasoning

1 teaspoon hot sauce, plus more to taste

2 teaspoons chopped fresh cilantro

Coarse salt, to taste

Yellow rice, for serving

1 Cut lobster tail into 4 pieces with shell intact. Heat 1 tablespoon olive oil in a sauté pan over medium. Add lobster pieces and sauté 5 minutes, or until mostly cooked through. Remove lobster from pan and keep warm.

2 In the same pan, add remaining olive oil and sauté peppers and onion over high heat for 3 minutes. Stir in tomatoes, Sazón seasoning, and hot sauce and bring to a simmer. Add lobster and heat through. Remove pan from heat and stir in cilantro. Season with salt. Serve hot with yellow rice.

LUIS GARCIA *and* MARÍA LUISA GARCIA

KAYE HURT'S LINGUINE with CLAM SAUCE

| SERVES 4 |

"I'M A FARMER, NOT A FISHERMAN," says Barry Hurt, scooping up a handful of baby clams no bigger than the head of a pin.

Hurt's clam farm sits on Placida Bay along the stretch of road heading out to Boca Grande on Florida's West Coast, where millions of tiny fertilized seeds from the hatchery are set on fine screens in a nursery and continuously fed for about three months with plankton-rich water from the bay.

Once the clams are about the size of a pea, Barry places them in mesh bags and takes them out to the state-owned bay bottom that he leases just offshore in about eight feet of open water. There he plants the tiny young clams on the sandy bottom in the bags designed to protect them from predators, such as blue crabs and stingrays, as they dig and grow to maturity. It will be almost two years before this generation is old enough to harvest.

Clams are big business on both the East and the West Coasts of Florida, with about 350 clam farmers in the state raising clams with no chemicals, antibiotics, or feeds. Barry is one of the few who are reviving sunray Venus clams, a native species that disappeared back in the 1940s, when clammers raked them in by the ton. Eventually, the harvest dwindled and the clams became nearly extinct. "They're beauties," Barry says, "and restaurant chefs love them because they make such a pretty plate." The meat is sweeter, too, he says.

Florida clams are harvested year-round in a variety of sizes: littleneck, middleneck, and pastaneck (the smallest). Barry's wife, Kaye, says her favorite way to serve clams is with a big pile of al dente linguine with fresh basil and a splash of Pernod. Kaye prefers tender littleneck clams (10 to 13 per pound) for this classic dish.

¼ cup extra-virgin olive oil

1 cup finely chopped sweet onion

6 garlic cloves, finely chopped

½ cup butter

Juice of 1 lemon, or to taste

1 ounce anise liqueur, such as Pernod

8 basil leaves, torn

1 cup bottled clam juice

2 pounds fresh littleneck clams, scrubbed

1 pound dried linguine

½ cup capers, for garnish

Freshly grated Parmesan cheese, for garnish

1 Warm olive oil in a large saucepan over medium heat. Add onions and garlic and cook until softened, about 3 minutes. Add butter and lemon juice and bring to a simmer. Stir in liqueur, basil, clam juice, and clams and simmer 8 to 10 minutes, or just until clams open.

2 Meanwhile, cook pasta according to package directions. Drain, then pour clam sauce over hot pasta and top with capers. Serve immediately with Parmesan cheese.

HOW TO CRACK A STONE CRAB CLAW

A COLOSSAL CLAW CAN WEIGH TWENTY-FIVE OUNCES OR MORE—THE CLAWS MAKE UP HALF THE WEIGHT OF THE WHOLE CRAB. IT TAKES TWELVE TO TWENTY-FOUR MONTHS TO REACH LEGAL SIZE AGAIN.

ARGUABLY THE BEST-KNOWN SEAFOOD RESTAURANT IN FLORIDA, Joe's Stone Crab in Miami Beach built its fame on the colossal claws of the Florida stone crab. Once considered too difficult to crack, they are now a sublime delicacy.

When Joe Weiss opened a lunch counter in 1913 serving fish sandwiches and fries, Miami Beach was just a swampy stretch of land. In 1918, Joe bought a bungalow, moved into the back with his wife, Jennie, set up tables on the front porch, and opened Joe's Restaurant.

The 1920s brought a building boom to the beach, and as his customer base grew, Joe figured out that the claws of the plentiful stone crabs in the bay could be boiled and cracked for the sweet white meat. He served them with hash browns, coleslaw, and mayonnaise, and Joe's Stone Crab was born.

Joe was pals with the likes of Will Rogers, Amelia Earhart, the Duke and Duchess of Windsor, Gloria Swanson, and J. Edgar Hoover, all of whom were regular patrons. Today's A-listers still clamor for a table, as the restaurant does not accept reservations.

Stone crabs are one of the most sustainable seafoods in Florida, harvested from October to May by removing just one claw. (Crabs are returned to the water, and their claws regenerate.) The restaurant has its own fleet of fishing boats and captures the crabs in baited traps. A colossal claw can weigh twenty-five ounces or more—the claws make up half the weight of the whole crab. It takes twelve to twenty-four months to reach legal size again.

And you know they're experts at cracking the claws in this kitchen—the restaurant serves up to 2,000 dinners on a busy night and ships this taste of Florida to fans around the world.

With three expertly placed cracks, you're ready to eat the sweet, succulent claw meat. Here's how it's done at Joe's:

1. Before cracking, place the claw on a cutting board or other hard surface. Place a plastic bag over the claw to keep crab juice from splattering.

2. Take a mallet or hammer and lightly crack the claw in spots 1 and 2, and slightly harder in spot 3.

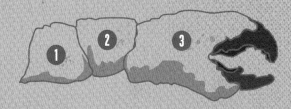

3. Next, peel the shells from the claw and then separate the two knuckles from the main pincher. Note that there is a hard center membrane inside the meat, so when biting into the meat, be careful. Treat the claw as if you were eating an artichoke, pulling the meat off the center.

4. Crack only as many as you can eat at one time.

PAN-FRIED HOGFISH

| SERVES 4 |

1½ cups panko (Japanese breadcrumbs)

2 teaspoons coarse salt

2 teaspoons finely grated fresh lemon zest

1 teaspoon dried dill

½ teaspoon freshly ground black pepper

3 eggs

3 tablespoons milk or water

2 pounds hogfish fillets, cut into 4 equal pieces

3 tablespoons light olive oil

Lemon wedges, for serving

BRETT WALLIN GREW UP WITH A FISHING ROD, on the water almost every day with his dad, Tom, part of a family of fishermen who started back in the early 1900s with Brett's great-great-great grandfather Claus Wallin, who hopped on a Ringling Circus train in the Northeast and ended up on Florida's West Coast.

The Wallin boys fished the waters around Sarasota with the seasons, hauling in clams, mullet, scallops, crab, and oysters. They knew all the bayous where grouper and snapper were plentiful and opened a fish market to sell their catch. Brett's dad, Tom, started frying fish for sandwiches for surrounding businesses, launching Walt's Fish Market and Restaurant in 1967.

Tom passed away in 2006, and today Brett is part owner of the restaurant on the Tamiami Trail in Sarasota, but he's rarely at the market—instead, he's out in his boat by 6:00 a.m. and can tell you what's abundant in any season. Hogfish, a reef species that inhabit rocky bottoms, ledges, and reefs, is one of his favorite catches. Identified by its long, hoglike snout, it roots for small prey on the bottom, so is not commonly caught on hook and line, but by spearfishing.

The meat is delicate and white, with thin fillets that cook quickly. Walt's serves it in a variety of ways, but this crunchy panko-crusted preparation is a favorite, and this is our version.

1 Combine panko, salt, lemon zest, dried dill, and pepper in a large, shallow dish.

2 Whisk together eggs and milk or water in a separate large, shallow dish.

3 Dip fish into egg mixture, shaking off excess. Dip both sides of fish into panko, pressing lightly to help it adhere.

4 Heat oil in a nonstick skillet over medium-high heat. Add fish, 2 pieces at a time, cooking until golden brown on both sides, 3 to 4 minutes per side, depending on thickness of fillets.

5 Serve hot with lemon wedges.

KALE SLAW with OVEN-ROASTED TOMATOES

SERVES 4

1 tablespoon finely grated fresh lemon zest

2 tablespoons fresh lemon juice

1 garlic clove, finely grated

2 anchovies, finely minced, or 1 tablespoon anchovy paste

¼ cup plus 1 tablespoon extra-virgin olive oil, plus additional for brushing

1 large bunch Tuscan kale, center stalks removed, cut into thin strips

1 pint small tomatoes, halved

Coarse salt, to taste

2 (1-inch-thick) slices sourdough bread

KALE SEEMS TO BE EVERYWHERE THESE DAYS, and for good reason. It's delicious, super-healthy, and easy to grow. The most important step to enjoying raw kale is massaging the leaves in the dressing and letting it sit long enough to soften up just a bit. This is a tender slaw that's great to take along on boat rides or camping trips because it can be enjoyed at room temperature. If you do pack it up to go, keep the croutons separate until you're ready to dig in.

1 Combine lemon zest, lemon juice, garlic, and anchovies in a large bowl. Whisk in one-quarter cup oil until well combined. Add kale, massaging leaves in dressing. Set aside.

2 Preheat oven to 400°F. Toss tomatoes with 1 tablespoon oil and sprinkle with salt. Place tomatoes on a large baking sheet and roast 20 minutes, until soft. Leave oven on.

3 Brush bread with olive oil and sprinkle with salt. Place on a baking sheet and bake 5 minutes, or until golden brown and crisp. Cut into cubes.

4 Top kale with tomatoes and croutons, tossing to combine.

PEA SHOOTS with RADISHES and CUCUMBERS

| SERVES 4 |

PEA SHOOTS ARE THE YOUNG LEAVES AND SPROUTS of the pea plant. They have a sweet nuttiness that is a tasty counterpoint to the spice of fresh, crunchy radishes. This simple recipe works well as a side dish to almost anything and comes together in minutes.

1 tablespoon white balsamic vinegar

¼ cup extra-virgin olive oil

5 cups pea shoots

1 medium watermelon radish, diced

½ cucumber, peeled, seeded, and thinly sliced

Coarse salt and coarsely ground black pepper, to taste

1 Whisk together vinegar and oil in a large bowl until well combined.

2 Add pea shoots, radish, and cucumber, tossing to combine. Sprinkle generously with salt and pepper before serving.

CITRUS SALAD with FENNEL and HEARTS OF PALM

| SERVES 4 |

2 red grapefruits

2 navel oranges

2 small fennel bulbs, cored and very thinly sliced

2 (14-ounce) cans hearts of palm, drained and thinly sliced

1 tablespoon fresh lemon juice

½ teaspoon coarse salt

¼ teaspoon freshly ground black pepper

¼ teaspoon ground cardamom

3 tablespoons extra-virgin olive oil

2 tablespoons thinly sliced fresh basil

LOOK FOR FENNEL BULBS THAT ARE UNBLEMISHED AND FIRM. To core the fennel, cut in half and use a sharp paring knife to cut out the hard white center. If you have a mandoline or V-slicer, now is the time to use it—fennel can be slightly tough, so the thinner you can slice it, the better.

1 Cut the skin and white pith from the grapefruits and oranges using a thin, sharp knife. Place a large bowl on a work surface. Cut between membranes in grapefruits and oranges to release segments into bowl. Place segments in a separate shallow bowl and squeeze membranes over large bowl to extract juice. Reserve 2 tablespoons citrus juice and set aside.

2 Combine citrus segments, fennel, and hearts of palm in the shallow bowl; set aside.

3 Combine lemon juice, salt, pepper, cardamom, and reserved citrus juice in a medium bowl. Whisk in olive oil until combined. Stir in basil.

4 Pour dressing over citrus mixture, tossing gently to coat. Serve immediately.

AUNT GLO'S FRIED GREEN TOMATOES

| SERVES 4 |

AUNT GLO WAS A SPITFIRE OF A LADY. Less than five feet tall and as thin as a rail, she always had twice the energy of anyone else around. Auntie to Pam and Katie, Glo was one of those cooks whose love was clearly evident in her food. Most of the classic dishes she made were painstaking and laborious, but with every succulent bite, you were thankful she took the time. Katie's childhood memories are infused with the foods Aunt Glo lovingly made. She and her husband, Web, would host the whole family at their humble Kissimmee home throughout the summer, and the spread was never complete without a platter piled high with Aunt Glo's fried green tomatoes—perhaps the simplest of all her recipes. Besides being a wonderful cook, she was a wonderful person. Katie's daughter carries on her name, and this simple recipe carries on her culinary legacy.

These are an ideal side for any kind of seafood dish, particularly fried shrimp. The secret to Aunt Glo's tomatoes is their thinness. You should almost be able to see through the tomatoes. If you slice them any thicker than ⅛ inch, the batter won't adhere.

Light olive oil or vegetable shortening, for frying

⅓ cup all-purpose flour

⅔ cup finely ground yellow cornmeal or cornmeal mix

3 large green tomatoes

Coarse salt and lots of ground black pepper

1 Add enough oil or shortening to reach ½ inch up sides of a large sauté pan or skillet. Heat over medium heat until oil shimmers.

2 Combine flour and cornmeal in a shallow dish; set aside. Slice tomatoes into ⅛ inch-thick slices. Dredge tomato slices in flour and cornmeal, covering completely. Knock off excess flour.

3 Add tomatoes, a few at a time, to hot oil, cooking until tomato is tender and crust is golden, about 3 minutes per side.

4 Drain on a plate lined with paper towels, season generously with salt and pepper. Serve warm.

GOODRICH'S ONION RINGS

SERVES 4 TO 6

6 cups canola oil

2 cups cold water

2 cups all-purpose flour

1 tablespoon coarse salt

2 cups panko (Japanese breadcrumbs)

2 large sweet white onions, peeled and cut into ¼- to ½-inch-thick rounds

Coarse salt

WHEN A JAMES BEARD–NOMINATED CHEF recommends a seafood joint, we take note. And when Disney's chef, Scott Hunnel, told us to make sure we tried the onion rings, among other things, at Goodrich Seafood and Oyster House in Oak Hill, we knew that was a recipe to share.

The Goodrich Seafood story starts in 1910, when brothers Jeff and Clarence Goodrich opened a wholesale seafood house and blue crab–processing facility about 300 feet from where the restaurant stands today. Independent crabbers sold their catch to the Goodriches, and employees, mostly women, picked the crabmeat after the crabs were steamed in a large coal- and wood-fired pressure steamer.

By 1969, state regulations had tightened and wooden floors were no longer allowed, so the old seafood plant closed. A new B. F. Goodrich & Son Seafood Company opened in the 1970s, known for nightly "oyster parties" and as a hangout for boaters and locals.

Today, plenty of fans still arrive by boat to sit on the back porch over the water at Goodrich Seafood and Oyster House and chow down on local specialties such as blue crab cakes, mullet, oysters, frog legs, and catch of the day (fried, of course). And a paper-lined basket of these onion rings is on nearly every table. Double dipping the onion rings makes them spectacularly crunchy. We use sweet Vidalia onions.

1 Heat oil to 375°F in a large pot. Place water, flour seasoned with salt, and panko into 3 medium shallow bowls. Line a baking sheet with paper towels to drain the onion rings as they come out of the oil.

2 Dip each onion ring in water, then flour, back in water, then in panko. Working in small batches, lower onion rings into oil one at a time using a slotted spoon or tongs. They should bubble slightly and then gradually rise to the top.

3 Fry until light brown, 1 to 2 minutes. Transfer to the prepared baking sheet to drain and continue frying onions in small batches. Season with salt and serve immediately.

KEY LIME MOUSSE and SHORTBREAD PARFAITS

| SERVES 6 |

THIS DESSERT IS A NICE DEPARTURE from the heavier cakes and cookies we usually eat in the wintertime. Bright citrus is in peak season when the weather is coldest. You can, of course, use regular limes here, but there's something special about those little golf ball–sized key limes and their sweet-tart flavor.

5 egg yolks

½ cup sugar

⅓ cup key lime juice

1 stick butter, cut in pieces and chilled

1 cup heavy cream

12 small purchased shortbread cookies, such as Lorna Doone or Pepperidge Farm Chessmen

1 Fill a medium saucepan with a few inches of water and place over medium-high heat.

2 Combine egg yolks and sugar in a heatproof bowl that's slightly bigger than the saucepan. Place bowl atop saucepan to create a double boiler and whisk yolks 1 minute. Add key lime juice and whisk 6 to 8 minutes, or until mixture thickens.

3 Remove pan from heat and add butter 1 piece at a time, stirring until fully melted before adding next piece.

4 Cool mixture to room temperature, then refrigerate until cold, about 4 hours.

5 Whip heavy cream until firm peaks form. Gently fold whipped cream into lime mixture until just combined. (A few streaks of whipped cream may remain.)

6 Spoon 3 tablespoons key lime mousse into the bottom of a serving glass. Crumble 1 shortbread cookie on mousse. Repeat with 3 tablespoons mousse, a second crumbled cookie, and finish with 2 tablespoons mousse.

SOUR ORANGE PIE

| SERVES 8 |

IN THE LATE 1970S, CAPT. JOHN A. BOLLMAN bought the property that is now home to J.B.'s Fish Camp in New Smyrna Beach. In those days, the site was home to a simple screened-in building. There was no kitchen, but lots of bait and beer. John originally named the place the Turtle Mound Raw Bar. He stored clams, oysters, and crabs and kept live shrimp inside the building. Selling bait and renting boats drove the business.

On the weekends, John roasted oysters and clams for customers. Eventually, he added commercial equipment and expanded his offerings to fried seafood and crab cakes. By 1987, the restaurant was called J.B.'s Fish Camp and had a new kitchen, more seats, and a new deck and dock.

It's the kind of place you go when you want no wine list, brown paper for table linens, and an ambience enriched by the smell of Skin-So-Soft or Cutter's insect repellent when the evening light dims. People come to J.B.'s to stare at a river and study its current, eat a simple supper, watch a sunset, sip on a lime-laced beverage, and marvel at the grace of a blue heron. And sometimes a rickety picnic table at the water's edge makes the most wonderful dining room.

Though J.B.'s wouldn't part with the recipe for its popular sour orange pie, a riff on the classic key lime, Donna Shelley of Mount Dora is renowned for her homemade cakes and pies, and this dessert is one of her favorites. We call for a store-bought piecrust for ease of preparation, but a chocolate graham cracker crust also works. Sour oranges can be hard to find in the grocery store, so check with your neighbors—the trees grow throughout the state and many are in residential backyards.

1 store-bought piecrust

4 large eggs, at room temperature, separated

1 (14-ounce) can sweetened condensed milk

1 teaspoon grated sour orange zest

¾ cup fresh sour orange juice

2 tablespoons extra-fine sugar

1 Preheat oven to 350°F. Line crust with foil and fill with dry beans or pie weights. Bake 5 minutes, or until golden; set aside to cool completely.

2 Mix egg yolks and sweetened condensed milk in a medium bowl. Fold in orange zest and juice.

3 Pour mixture into cooled pie shell and bake for 10 minutes.

4 Whip egg whites into a froth, then gradually add sugar. Beat until stiff peaks form. Spread over warm pie crust to seal edges. Bake until meringue is golden. Chill and serve.

YEAR-ROUND
Sauces
& ACCESSORIES

RÉMOULADES • MIGNONETTES • SAUCES • GLAZES • BUTTERS • RÉMOULADES • MIGNONETTES • S

THIS CHAPTER CONTAINS WHAT WE LIKE TO CALL "ACCESSORIES"—
SAUCES AND SUCH THAT ACCENT SIMPLY PREPARED SEAFOOD.

THESE SAUCES COME TOGETHER QUICKLY a[...]

shellfish or a simple piece of fish to somethin[...]

GREEN OLIVE SALSA VERDE

| MAKES ABOUT 1½ CUPS |

1 cup loosely packed fresh parsley leaves

½ cup chopped green olives

2 tablespoons capers

1 heaping tablespoon finely grated fresh lemon zest

1 tablespoon fresh lemon juice

⅓ cup extra-virgin olive oil

Coarse salt and red pepper flakes, to taste

1 Make a mound of parsley, olives, capers, and lemon zest on a large cutting board. Chop together until everything is pretty finely chopped.

2 Scrape mixture into a medium bowl. Stir in lemon juice until combined, then stir in olive oil. Season to taste with salt and red pepper flakes. Refrigerate, covered, at least 3 hours and up to overnight before serving.

CITRUS-TARRAGON GLAZE

| MAKES 1 CUP |

½ teaspoon mustard powder

¼ cup freshly squeezed lemon juice

½ cup orange marmalade

2 tablespoons chopped fresh tarragon

Coarse salt and freshly ground black pepper, to taste

Combine all ingredients in small saucepan over medium heat. Cook, stirring constantly, until well combined and mixture begins to thicken, 5 to 7 minutes.

ORANGE-SAFFRON BEURRE BLANC

| MAKES ABOUT ¾ CUP |

1 Combine wine, orange juice, shallot, and saffron in a medium heavy saucepan over medium heat; bring to a boil and cook until liquid is syrupy and reduced, about 5 minutes.

2 Add cream, salt, and pepper and boil 1 minute.

3 Reduce heat to medium-low and add a few tablespoons butter, whisking constantly. Add remaining butter a few pieces at a time, whisking constantly and adding new pieces before previous ones have completely liquefied, removing pan from heat occasionally to cool mixture.

4 Remove pan from heat. Season to taste with salt and pepper and pour sauce through a fine-mesh sieve into a small bowl. Discard shallot and saffron. Serve immediately.

¼ cup dry white wine

¼ cup fresh orange juice

2 tablespoons finely chopped shallot

Generous pinch saffron threads

⅓ cup heavy cream

¼ teaspoon salt

⅛ teaspoon freshly ground black pepper

2 sticks cold unsalted butter, cut into tablespoon-sized pieces

COCKTAIL SAUCES ARE TRADITIONALLY SERVED as a dip for steamed, boiled, or fried seafood. They are a popular condiment for good reason: they're spicy, sassy, and easy on the eyes.

CLASSIC COCKTAIL SAUCE

| MAKES ABOUT 1¼ CUPS |

1 cup ketchup

¼ teaspoon orange zest

2 tablespoons fresh lemon juice

1 to 2 tablespoons prepared horseradish

Dash Worcestershire sauce

Few drops hot sauce

Coarse salt, to taste

Combine all ingredients, cover, and refrigerate until ready to use.

SPICY POMEGRANATE COCKTAIL SAUCE

| MAKES ABOUT 1 CUP |

⅔ cup pomegranate seeds

⅔ cup chili sauce, such as Heinz

1 tablespoons smoked paprika

1 tablespoon Worcestershire sauce

1 teaspoon sriracha sauce

1 teaspoon fresh lemon juice

1 teaspoon prepared horseradish

Coarse salt, to taste

Purée all ingredients in food processor until smooth. Strain through a fine-mesh sieve into a small bowl to remove any bits of pomegranate seed. Cover and refrigerate until ready to use.

GREEN GODDESS COCKTAIL SAUCE

| MAKES 1½ CUPS |

Purée all ingredients in food processor until smooth. Cover and refrigerate until ready to use.

½ cup sour cream

⅓ cup mayonnaise

3 tablespoons chopped fresh parsley

2 tablespoons chopped fresh chives

3 tablespoons chopped fresh tarragon

1 tablespoon rice vinegar

1 tablespoon fresh lemon juice

1 tablespoon anchovy paste

Coarse salt and freshly ground black pepper, to taste

RÉMOULADES ARE ESSENTIALLY A FRENCH VERSION of tartar sauce. They are great as a dip for shellfish or as a spread for sandwiches.

HERB RÉMOULADE

| MAKES 1 CUP |

1 cup mayonnaise

3 tablespoons minced fresh chives, tarragon, parsley, or chervil, or a combination

2 tablespoons Creole mustard

1 tablespoon capers, rinsed and chopped

Anchovy paste, to taste

½ teaspoon sweet Hungarian paprika

Hot sauce, to taste

Coarse pepper, to taste

Combine all ingredients in small bowl. Refrigerate, covered, at least 2 hours before serving, or overnight.

LEMON RÉMOULADE

| MAKES ABOUT 2½ CUPS |

1½ cups mayonnaise

1 teaspoon finely grated fresh lemon zest

2 tablespoons fresh lemon juice

2 tablespoons white wine vinegar

1½ tablespoons Dijon mustard

2 tablespoons prepared creamy horseradish, or to taste

1 tablespoon chopped fresh parsley

1 teaspoon smoked paprika

¼ teaspoon cayenne pepper

¼ cup finely chopped celery

¼ cup finely chopped green onions, white and green parts

1 tablespoon capers, rinsed and drained, optional

Hot sauce, to taste

Combine all ingredients in a small bowl. Cover and refrigerate overnight.

MIGNONETTES ARE A CLASSIC CONDIMENT FOR RAW OYSTERS and can be used as a dip or sprinkled directly onto the oyster in the shell before eating. With a spicy bite from raw onion and a little pucker from vinegar, these sauces beautifully enhance the oyster's flavor.

CUCUMBER-WATERMELON MIGNONETTE GRANITA
| MAKES ½ CUP |

½ cup white wine vinegar

½ cup watermelon juice

¼ cup grated cucumber

2 tablespoons minced shallot

1 teaspoon prepared horseradish

¼ teaspoon coarse salt

1 Combine vinegar, watermelon juice, cucumber, shallot, horseradish, and salt in a medium bowl, stirring until salt dissolves. Cover and refrigerate overnight.

2 Strain through a fine-mesh sieve, discarding solids. Pour strained mixture into a container big enough to fit mixture in a thin layer. Freeze until mixture begins to freeze around edges, 30 to 45 minutes. Scrape with a fork to break up ice crystals.

3 Continue freezing and stirring with a fork every hour or so until mixture is completely frozen. Use a fork to scrape into flaky crystals.

ASIAN MIGNONETTE
| MAKES ½ CUP |

½ cup rice vinegar

3 green onions, white and light green parts, finely minced

1 bird's-eye chile pepper, finely minced

1 teaspoon minced fresh cilantro

½ teaspoon fish sauce

Combine vinegar and minced green onion in a medium bowl. Set aside 15 minutes. Stir in chile, cilantro, and fish sauce, stirring to combine. Refrigerate 20 minutes before serving.

CHAMPAGNE–PINK PEPPERCORN MIGNONETTE

| MAKES ½ CUP |

Combine vinegar and minced shallot in a medium bowl. Set aside 15 minutes. Stir in peppercorns, dill, and salt, stirring until salt dissolves. Refrigerate 20 minutes before serving.

¼ cup champagne vinegar

1 tablespoon minced shallot

2 teaspoons pink peppercorns, coarsely crushed

1 teaspoon minced fresh dill

¼ teaspoon fine sea salt

Splash of dry champagne

COMPOUND BUTTERS ARE ALMOST "STUPID EASY," as our friend Helen Miller likes to say. They pack a ton of flavor carried by silky butter and could probably make shoe leather taste great. We recommend a dollop on top of fish fillets before baking in parchment paper or melted on top of lobster tails just before they come off the grill.

AVOCADO BUTTER

| MAKES ABOUT ½ CUP |

½ cup unsalted butter, softened

2 small ripe Haas avocados, peeled and mashed

2 tablespoons fresh lemon juice

2 tablespoons finely minced fresh cilantro

1 jalapeño pepper, seeded and finely minced

2 teaspoons ground cumin

Hot sauce, to taste

Coarse salt and freshly ground black pepper, to taste

1 Combine softened butter with other ingredients in a mixing bowl until completely blended.

2 Spoon onto parchment paper or plastic wrap. Roll into a log, using the edge of a baking sheet to form a tight log. Chill for 2 hours before serving. Store refrigerated, or freeze for up to 6 months.

HABANERO-LIME-TEQUILA BUTTER

| MAKES ABOUT ½ CUP |

½ cup unsalted butter, softened

½ teaspoon finely minced habanero pepper

1 tablespoon fresh lime juice

2 teaspoons tequila

1 teaspoon coarse salt

1 Combine softened butter with other ingredients in a mixing bowl until completely blended.

2 Spoon onto parchment paper or plastic wrap. Roll into a log, using the edge of a baking sheet to form a tight log. Chill for 2 hours before serving. Store refrigerated, or freeze for up to 6 months.

ORANGE-PARSLEY BUTTER

½ cup unsalted butter, softened

2 tablespoons finely minced
fresh parsley

1 tablespoon orange zest

2 teaspoons freshly ground
black pepper

1 teaspoon coarse salt

1 Combine softened butter with
other ingredients in a mixing
bowl until completely blended.

2 Spoon onto parchment paper
or plastic wrap. Roll into a log,
using the edge of a baking sheet
to form a tight log. Chill for
2 hours before serving. Store
refrigerated, or freeze for up to
6 months.

FLORIDA'S HISTORIC FISHING VILLAGES

FOR THOUSANDS OF YEARS, people in Florida have made their living from the Gulf of Mexico, the Atlantic Ocean, and inland waterways. Their connection with the water has shaped the state's past and present and will doubtless shape its future. Waterfront communities have experienced dramatic cycles of boom and bust, but these small towns still reflect Florida's rich heritage.

APALACHICOLA

More than 900 homes, buildings, and sites in the city's historic district have been named a "distinctive destination" by the National Trust for Historic Preservation. The warm, shallow waters of the bay are still a productive marine ecosystem, with plump oysters that have made Apalachicola famous around the world.

CEDAR KEY

Clam aquaculture thrives in this charming fishing village, which was a major supplier of seafood and timber products to the northeast in the late 1800s. (Cedar Key is named for the eastern red cedar, which once grew abundantly in the area.)

CORTEZ

Two-square-mile Cortez is one of the few remaining working waterfronts on Florida's Sun Coast. Fish houses, such as the Star Fish Co., opened in the 1920s, still serve delicious fresh catches, while N. E. Taylor Boatworks, tracing it lineage to 1928, still keeps the boats running.

FERNANDINA

Amelia Island and the seaport village of Fernandina are often called the birthplace of the shrimp industry. Today you'll still find locally caught shrimp and a downtown lined with nineteenth-century Victorian homes and historic buildings.

KEY WEST

The southernmost point in the United States was discovered by Ponce de León in 1513, became a Spanish colony, and was deeded to the United States in the 1800s. Old Town, the original Key West neighborhood, has classic wooden bungalows and mansions dating from 1886 to 1912.

ST. MARKS

This coastal community on the St. Marks and Wakulla Rivers is one of the oldest in Florida, with almost 500 years of European-American history. One of Florida's first railroads connected St. Marks with Tallahassee in 1836.

SEBASTIAN

Traces of Sebastian's eighteenth-century culture can be found in area history and archaeology museums. The riverfront of one of Florida's authentic Treasure Coast towns is home to classic fish houses, dockside restaurants, and a marina, and the Old Town Sebastian Historic District West contains fifteen historic buildings.

STEINHATCHEE

Steinhatchee (STEEN hatch-ee) originally was known as Deadman Bay, then Stephensville. In 1931, the name was changed to Steinhatchee after the river with the same name. The name derives from the Native American *esteen hatchee*, meaning river (*hatchee*) of man (*esteen*). Today Steinhatchee is a prime scalloping destination with marinas and fishing camps.

TARPON SPRINGS

On the National Register of Historic Places, this little city was named for the abundant tarpon in surrounding waters, but it is best known as "the sponge capital of the world."

Pensacola

Fort Walton Beach

Tallahassee

Panama City

Port St Joe

FLORIDA

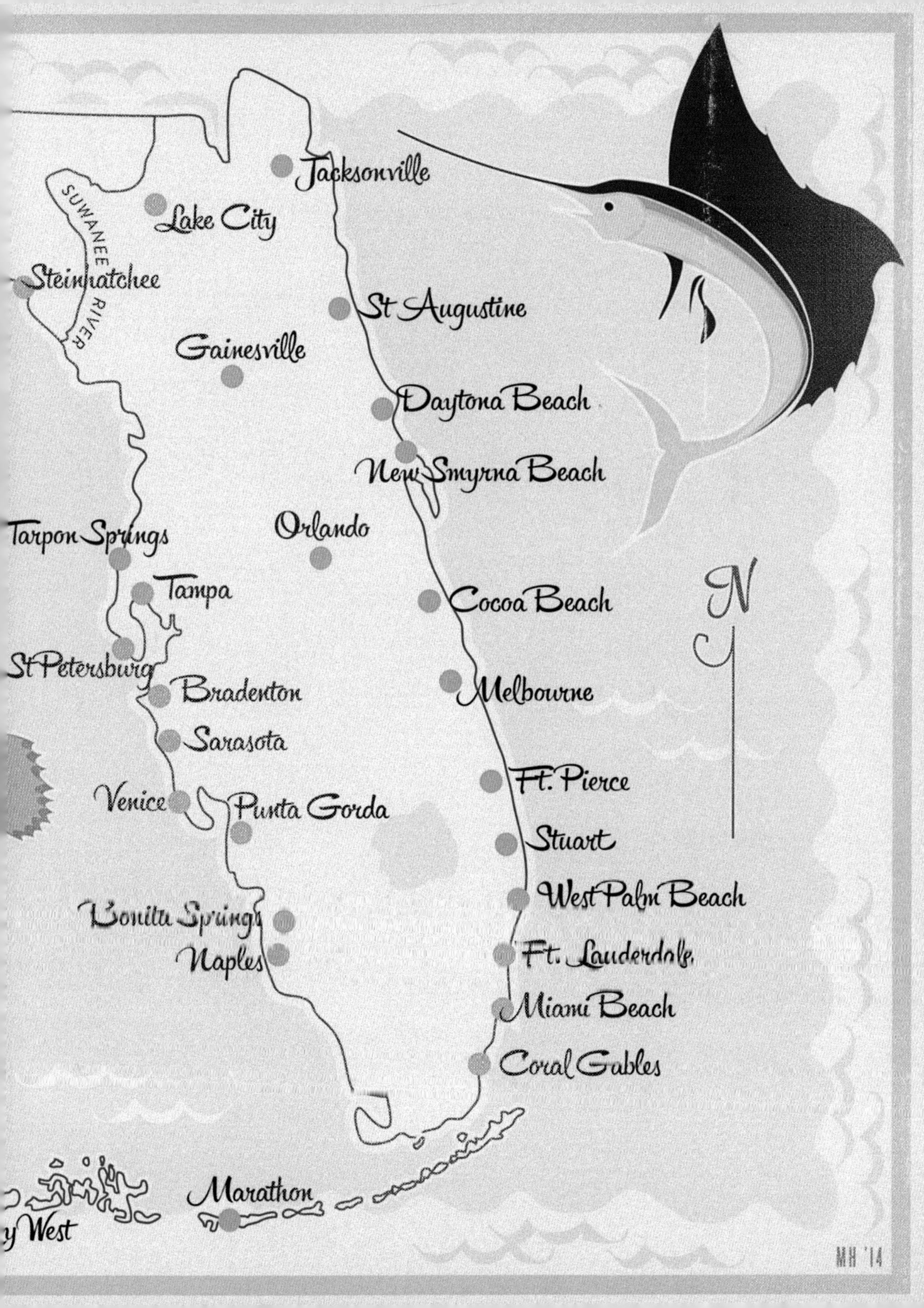

Jacksonville

Lake City

SUWANEE RIVER

Steinhatchee

Gainesville

St Augustine

Daytona Beach

New Smyrna Beach

Tarpon Springs

Orlando

Tampa

Cocoa Beach

St Petersburg

Bradenton

Melbourne

Sarasota

Venice

Punta Gorda

Ft. Pierce

Stuart

West Palm Beach

Bonita Springs

Ft. Lauderdale

Naples

Miami Beach

Coral Gables

Key West

Marathon

N

MH '14

SEAFOOD AT A GLANCE

HERE'S A CLOSER LOOK at the seafood we include in this book.

FRESHWATER FISH

AMERICAN SHAD: Found mostly in the St. Johns River and Nassau River when it returns from the ocean to spawn. Roe is also eaten.

CATFISH: Found in big rivers and in the lower reaches of major tributaries. Channel, blue, and white catfish are preferred by most cooks for their creamy, sweet flesh.

SALTWATER FISH

COBIA: Found in near-shore and inshore waters with inlets and bays. Cobia are frequently found around buoys, pilings, and wrecks in these areas. Excellent table fare.

DRUM: Black and red drum are edible, with a moderate flavor, and are not oily.

FLOUNDER: Gulf flounder are found inshore on sandy or mud bottoms and are often found in tidal creeks. They may also be caught occasionally on near-shore rocky reefs.

GROUPER: Prized species with a mild, sweet flesh. Varieties include red, black, gag, yellowmouth, yellowtail, Warsaw, and gray. Goliath and Nassau varieties are protected.

JACKS: Wide-ranging variety that includes banded rudderfish, crevalle, and amberjack.

MACKEREL: Cero variety is found near shore and offshore fish mainly in South Florida. Spanish mackerel prevalent throughout Florida waters.

MAHI MAHI: Also called a dolphin fish. The flesh is creamy and clean tasting. The United States and the Caribbean countries are the primary consumers of this fish. »

MULLET: Fantail mullet spawn in near-shore and possibly inshore waters during spring and summer. Striped are commonly found inshore.

POMPANO: Common in inshore and near-shore waters, especially along sandy beaches and oyster banks and over grass beds.

SEA TROUT: Sand sea trout are a Gulf species that may occur in the Atlantic waters of extreme southeastern Florida. Silver sea trout are most common over sand or sandy mud bottoms offshore along both the Gulf and the Atlantic Coasts of Florida.

SHEEPSHEAD: An inshore species commonly found around oyster bars, seawalls, and in tidal creeks.

SNAPPER: Varieties include red, cubera, dog, lane, mahogany, queen, silk, yellowtail, vermilion, and mutton.

SNOOK: An inshore species found in mangrove habitats. Varieties include swordspine, small-scaled fat snook, large-scaled fat snook, and common and tarpon snook.

STURGEON: The free-flowing, spring-fed Suwannee River supports the largest and most robust population of Gulf sturgeon in the state and the wider Gulf of Mexico region. The meat and roe are prized.

SWORDFISH: Deep-sea fish found from the surface to below 2,000 feet. They are heavily overfished internationally. Meaty, firm-fleshed fish.

TRIPLETAIL: Elongated fins make tripletail appear to have three tails. Inhabits inshore, near shore, and offshore waters. Meat is white, sweet, and flaky, similar to grouper.

SHELLFISH

BLUE CRAB: Harvested and eaten in two stages of its life cycle: when the exoskeleton is hard, and also when it's soft. Delicate, sweet meat is available fresh or pasteurized.

CLAMS: Florida hard clams are harvested year-round and are always available in steady supply. Though some clams are still wild caught, clam farming is a growing industry. »

CONCH: Queen conch once constituted significant commercial and recreational fisheries in Florida. In 1975, the commercial fishery was closed because of overfishing. In 1985, this ban was extended to the recreational fishery in state waters. In 1986, the state of Florida began a research program designed to monitor the recovery of the conch stock and determine how best to rehabilitate the depleted population.

OYSTERS: Available year-round, but harvest gears up in fall as water temperatures begin to drop. During cool months, oysters taste the best.

ROCK SHRIMP: Rock shrimp occur from about Norfolk, Virginia, south throughout the Gulf of Mexico to Cabo Catoche, Yucatán. The flavor is sweet and more akin to lobster than to shrimp.

SCALLOPS: Bay scallops live in shallow, near-shore waters along Florida's Gulf Coast, from Pensacola to the Florida Keys.

SHRIMP: Florida harvests four species of commercial-value shrimp—pink, brown, white, and royal red. Most shrimp harvested in Florida are the pink type.

SPINY LOBSTER: Crustacean related to crabs, shrimp, crawfish, and the Spanish lobster. Caught off the Keys and around the southern tip of the state in the Atlantic Ocean.

STONE CRAB: Fishery is closed five months each year to protect and sustain the crab. The stone crab's ability to regenerate lost limbs makes it possible to harvest the meaty claws without killing the crab.

OTHER

ALLIGATOR: A lean meat that is low in fat and cholesterol and high in protein. It is available in a variety of cuts, including tail meat fillets, ribs, nuggets, and wings. Tail meat, the choicest cut, is a mild-flavored white meat that has a texture similar to that of veal. Ribs, nuggets, and wings are darker meat with a stronger taste and a texture similar to that of pork shoulder.

Sources: Florida Department of Agriculture and Consumer Services; Florida Fish and Wildlife Conservation Commission; Monterey Bay Aquarium Foundation

FROG LEGS: Rich in protein, omega-3 fatty acids, vitamin A, and potassium. Mild flavor is similar to chicken and texture akin to chicken wings.

OCTOPUS: Flavorful meat; can be eaten raw, grilled, pickled, or sautéed.

RECIPES AT A GLANCE

RESOURCES

Anna Maria Fish Co.
101 Pine Ave.
Anna Maria, FL 34216
(941) 778-8710
www.cortezbottarga.com

Boss Oyster
125 Water St.
Apalachicola, FL 32320
(850) 653-9364
apalachicolariverinn.com

BeckyJack's Food Shack
8070 Cortez Blvd.
Weeki Wachee, FL 34607
(352) 610-4412

Cheeca Lodge and Spa
81801 Overseas Hwy.
Islamorada, FL 33036
(305) 664-4651
www.cheeca.com

Conch House Marina Resort
57 Comares Ave.
St. Augustine, FL 32080
(904) 829-8646
www.conch-house.com

Deal's Famous Oyster House
2571 U.S. Hwy. 98
Perry, FL 32348
(850) 838-3325

Dixie Crossroads Seafood
1475 Garden St.
Titusville, FL 32796
(321) 268-5000
www.dixiecrossroads.com

Freezer Tiki Bar
5590 S. Boulevard Dr.
Homosassa, FL 34448
(352) 628-2452

Garcia's Seafood Grille and Fish Market
398 N.W. North River Dr.
Miami, FL 33128
(305) 375-0765
www.garciasmiami.com

Goodrich Seafood and Oyster House
253 River Rd.
Oak Hill, FL 32759
(386) 345-3397
www.goodrichseafood
andoysterhouse.com

Harry T's Lighthouse
46 Harbor Blvd.
Destin, FL 32541
(850) 654-4800
www.harryts.com

Indian Pass Raw Bar
8391 Indian Pass Rd.
Port St. Joe, FL 32456
(850) 227-1670
www.indianpassrawbar.com

J.B.'s Fish Camp
859 Pompano Ave.
New Smyrna Beach, FL 32169
(386) 427-5747
www.jbsfishcamp.com

Joe Patti's Seafood
524 S. B St.
Pensacola, FL 32502
(850) 432-3315
www.joepattis.com

Joe's Stone Crab
11 Washington Ave.
Miami Beach, FL 33139
(305) 673-0365
www.joesstonecrab.com

Key Largo Conch House
100211 Overseas Hwy.
Key Largo, FL 33037
(305) 453-4844
www.keylargoconchhouse.com

Keys Fisheries Market and Marina
3502 Gulfview Ave.
Marathon, FL 33050
(305) 743-4353
www.keysfisheries.com

O'Steen's
205 Anastasia Blvd.
St. Augustine, FL 32080
(904) 829-6974
www.osteensrestaurant.com

Peace River Seafood
5337 Duncan Rd.
Punta Gorda, FL 33982
(941) 505-8440

Peck's Old Port Cove
139 N. Ozello Tr.
Crystal River, FL 34429
(352) 795-2806

Singleton's Seafood Shack
4728 Ocean St.
Atlantic Beach, FL 32233
(904) 246-4442

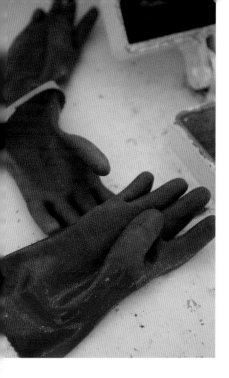

Stumpknockers on the River
13821 S.W. Hwy. 200
Dunnellon, FL 34432
(352) 854-2288
www.stumpknockersontheriver
.com

Ted Peters Famous Smoked Fish
1350 Pasadena Ave. South
St. Petersburg, FL 33707
(727) 381-7931
www.tedpetersfish.com

Walt's Fish Market and Restaurant
4144 Tamiami S. Tr.
Sarasota, FL 34231
(941) 921-4605
www.waltsfish.com

Wild Ocean Seafood Market
688 South Park Ave.
Titusville, FL 32796
(321) 269-1116
and
710 Bluewater Dr.
Port Canaveral, FL 32920
(321) 783-2300
www.wildoceanmarket.com

MISCELLANEOUS
Chokoloskee Charters
Capt. Charles Wright
P.O. Box 824
Chokoloskee Island, FL 34138
(239) 695-9107
www.chokoloskeecharters.com

Evans Fish Farm
Pierson, FL 32180
(386) 547-5066
www.evansfishfarm.com and
www.anastasiagoldcaviar.com

Everglades National Park
40001 State Road 9336
Homestead, FL 33034
www.npca.org/Everglades

Florida Department of
Agriculture and Consumer
Services, Division of Marketing
and Development
Bureau of Seafood and
Aquaculture Marketing
The Collins Building,
Innovation Park
2051 E. Dirac Dr.
Tallahassee, FL 32310
1-800-HELP-FLA
(1-800-435-7352)
www.freshfromflorida.com

Florida Fish and Wildlife
Conservation Commission
Farris Bryant Building
620 S. Meridian St.
Tallahassee, FL 32399-1600
www.myfwc.com

Halifax Historical Museum
252 S. Beach St.
Daytona Beach, FL 32114
(386) 255-6976
www.halifaxhistorical.org

Highland Park Fish Camp
2640 Highland Park Rd.
DeLand, FL 32720
(386) 734-2334
www.hpfishcamp.com

Chef Jamie McFadden
Cuisiniers Catered Cuisine
and Events
5470 Lake Howell Rd.
Winter Park, FL 32792
and
East End Market
3201 Corrine Dr.
Orlando, FL 32803
(407) 975-8763
www.cuisinierscater.com

Monterey Bay Aquarium
Foundation
866 Cannery Row
Monterey, CA 93940
(831) 648-4800
montereybayaquarium.org

Mote Marine Laboratory
1600 Ken Thompson Pkwy.
Sarasota, FL 34236
(941) 388-4441
www.mote.org

Rod and Gun Club
200 Riverside Dr.
Everglades City, FL 34139
(239) 695-2101
www.evergladesrodandgun.com

Sarasota Bay Estuary Program
111 S. Orange Ave.
Sarasota, FL 34236
(941) 955-8085
www.sarasotabay.org

APPENDIX OF FISH SUBSTITUTIONS

AMBERJACK: Firm texture, white meat with mild flavor; extra-lean fish. Substitute mahi mahi, mullet, tilefish, grouper; buy ¼- to ⅓-pound fillets per serving.

BLUE CRAB: Sweet, creamy meat; high in protein and low in fat. Substitute golden crab, rock shrimp, stone crab, spiny lobster, shrimp; buy 3 to 4 whole crabs per serving.

CLAMS: Firm texture; rich meat with sweet to slightly salty flavor; extra-lean. Substitute scallops or oysters; buy 6 whole clams per serving or ½ pint shucked clams per serving.

FLOUNDER: Firm white meat, delicate flake, fine texture, mild flavor; lean. Substitute red snapper; buy ¼- to ⅓-pound fillets per serving.

GROUPER: Firm texture; white meat with large flake and mild flavor; extra-lean. Substitute amberjack, snapper, mahi mahi, catfish, tilefish, tripletail; buy ¼- to ⅓-pound fillets per serving.

KING MACKEREL: Medium-firm texture; dark meat with full flavor; lean. Substitute Spanish mackerel, tuna, swordfish; buy ¼- to ⅓-pound fillets per serving.

MAHI MAHI: Firm texture; light, sweetly moist meat with solid flake and moderate flavor; extra-lean. Substitute amberjack, mullet, pompano, farm-raised catfish, grouper, tuna; buy ¼- to ⅓-pound fillets per serving.

MULLET: Firm texture; light meat with moderate flavor; lean. Substitute mahi mahi, pompano, Spanish mackerel, amberjack; buy ¼- to ⅓-pound fillets per serving.

OYSTERS: Tender to firm texture; flavor varies from salty to bland; extra-lean. Substitute clams; buy 6 whole oysters per serving or ⅓ to ½ pint shucked oysters per serving.

POMPANO: Firm texture; light meat with mild flavor; lean. Substitute mullet, mahi mahi, snapper; buy ¼- to ⅓-pound fillets per serving.

RED SNAPPER: Firm texture; white meat with mild flavor; lean. Substitute grouper, swordfish, tilefish, amberjack: buy ¼- to ⅓-pound fillets per serving.

SHRIMP: Crisp texture with sweet, distinct flavor; low fat. Substitute blue crab, spiny lobster, golden crab, rock shrimp; buy ⅓ pound headless and unpeeled shrimp per serving.

SPANISH MACKEREL: Medium-firm texture; dark meat with full flavor; lean. Substitute mullet, swordfish, king mackerel; buy ¼- to ⅓-pound fillets per serving.

SPINY LOBSTER: Firm texture; white meat with sweet, distinct flavor; low fat. Substitute blue crab, golden crab, rock shrimp, shrimp; buy 1 pound per serving.

STONE CRAB: Firm texture; sweet meat; very lean. Substitute golden crab, blue crab; buy 3 claws per person.

SWORDFISH: Firm texture; light meat with moderate flavor; extra-lean. Substitute tuna, king mackerel; buy ¼- to ⅓-pound fillets per serving.

TILEFISH: Firm, white meat with mild flavor; extra-lean. Substitute amberjack, grouper, snapper; buy ¼- to ⅓-pound fillets per serving.

YELLOWFIN TUNA: Firm, light meat with full flavor; lean. Substitute swordfish, mahi mahi, king mackerel; buy ¼- to ⅓-pound fillets per serving.

YELLOWTAIL SNAPPER: Firm texture; white meat with mild flavor; lean. Substitute grouper, swordfish, tilefish, amberjack; buy ¼- to ⅓-pound fillets per serving

ACKNOWLEDGMENTS

WE OFFER TREMENDOUS THANKS to our families for their infinite encouragement, and to the humble fishermen who took the time from their busy days to take us out on the water or sit around a table and tell us their stories.

We are ever so grateful to our trusted friends who tested and retested every recipe in this book: Stephanie Wood Hughes, Stephanie McAndrew, Karen Mills, Elissa Roesch, and Katie Wilson. Your thoughtful input has truly made the recipes shine.

Thanks to Diana Zalucky for gorgeous photos that help tell the story; to our gifted designer, Jason Farmand, who teamed up to bring the pages to life; and to Melissa Huerta for her stylish illustrations, which give the book even more personality.

Thanks to the Conrad Hilton Hotel in Miami and Cheeca Lodge in Islamorada for beautiful accommodations as we researched South Florida; to Jackie Kay Parker and Jamie McFadden of Cuisiniers for their expertise as we developed our beautiful Florida seafood boil (and fried frog legs).

We are grateful to the Sunnyland Chapter of the Antique and Classic Boat Society for helping us with photography.

Thanks to the University Press of Florida for our wonderful editors, Sian Hunter and Michele Fiyak-Burkley; design and production manager Lynn Werts, for keeping the book on track; and to publicist Teal Amthor-Shaffer, for spreading the word.

FROM PAM: To my husband, Steve, for his boundless support and partnership, and to my children for their love which keeps me going. To my sisters, Patti, Cathe, and Karen, who provide a safety net of love, and to friends who bring joy to each day.

FROM KATIE: Thanks times a million to my husband, Jason, for his patience, encouragement, and inspiring creativity, and to my beautiful Hazel, who keeps me grounded and lifts me up on a daily basis. Thanks, also, to my wonderful friends and family for being as excited about this book as I am.

FROM HEATHER: To my husband, Spencer, for his inspiration, encouragement, and spirit of adventure, and to my family and friends for their love and support. And to my coworkers and avid fishermen Mark Blythe and Hank Curtis for their guidance.

INDEX

Page numbers in *italics* indicate illustrations.

ADDITIONAL PHOTO CREDITS

All photographs not listed below are by Diana Zalucky.

Courtesy of Anna Maria Fish Company: page 127

Courtesy of Bob Brumback: 23

Courtesy of Cheeca Lodge: 143, 155

Courtesy of Everglades NPS: v, 156, 164–65, 262–63

Courtesy of the Halifax Historical Museum, Daytona Beach: 64

Rob Holland: 18

Courtesy of Brian Lockwood: 211

Courtesy of NASA: 79

Courtesy of the Orlando Sentinel: 96

Courtesy of Ponce de Leon Inlet Lighthouse Preservation Association: 107

Mike Shellen: 78

Courtesy of the State Archives of Florida: 63

PAM BRANDON is managing editor of *Edible Orlando* magazine and a food columnist for OrlandoSentinel.com and the *Palm Beach Post*. She has written twelve cookbooks, including *Field to Feast: Recipes Celebrating Florida Farmers, Chefs, and Artisans* and the *2014 Epcot International Food & Wine Festival Cookbook*. Her favorite Florida seafood, hands down, is wild-caught, crispy fried shrimp with a splash of lemon.

KATIE FARMAND, a proud Florida native, is an Orlando-based food writer, recipe developer, and food stylist. She is the editor of *Edible Orlando* magazine. She grew up deep-sea fishing with her grandparents and, to this day, a sandwich made with fried freshly caught grouper is her definition of perfection. This is her second cookbook.

HEATHER McPHERSON is the food editor and restaurant critic for the *Orlando Sentinel* and OrlandoSentinel.com. She is a past president of the Association of Food Journalists and is author of two cookbooks, coauthor of five cookbooks, and editor of three others. Her latest work is *Field to Feast: Recipes Celebrating Florida Farmers, Chefs, and Artisans* with Pam Brandon and Katie Farmand. She loves all Florida seafood, but grouper with a lemony caper-dill sauce is her favorite.

DIANA ZALUCKY is a Los Angeles–based photographer/director hailing from St. Thomas, U.S. Virgin Islands. She spent 10 years in Florida, where food photography became a passion. Diana loves narrating on set, playing in the mountains or ocean, and finding the good life wherever she goes.